IMAGES OF THE PAST

THE DISTRICT NURSE

A PICTORIAL HISTORY

IMAGES OF THE PAST

THE DISTRICT NURSE

A PICTORIAL HISTORY

SUSAN COHEN

PEN & SWORD
HISTORY

AN IMPRINT OF PEN & SWORD BOOKS LTD.
YORKSHIRE – PHILADELPHIA

First published in Great Britain in 2018 by
Pen & Sword History
An imprint of
Pen & Sword Books Ltd
Yorkshire - Philadelphia

Copyright © Susan Cohen, 2018

ISBN 978 1 47387 579 1

A CIP catalogue record for this book is available from the British Library.

Printed and bound in England
By CPI Group (UK) Ltd, Croydon, CR0 4YY

Pen & Sword Books Ltd incorporates the Imprints of Pen & Sword Books Archaeology, Atlas, Aviation, Battleground, Discovery, Family History, History, Maritime, Military, Naval, Politics, Railways, Select, Transport, True Crime, Fiction, Frontline Books, Leo Cooper, Praetorian Press, Seaforth Publishing, Wharncliffe and White Owl.

For a complete list of Pen & Sword titles please contact

PEN & SWORD BOOKS LIMITED
47 Church Street, Barnsley, South Yorkshire, S70 2AS, England
E-mail: enquiries@pen-and-sword.co.uk
Website: www.pen-and-sword.co.uk

or

PEN AND SWORD BOOKS
1950 Lawrence Rd, Havertown, PA 19083, USA
E-mail: Uspen-and-sword@casematepublishers.com
Website: www.penandswordbooks.com

Every attempt has been made by the Publishers to secure the appropriate permissions for materials reproduced in this book. If there has been any oversight we will be happy to amend this in any future editions.

CONTENTS

Foreword

I AM DELIGHTED to have been asked to write the foreword for this excellent new illustrated history of district nursing. I am also thrilled that the Queen's Nursing Institute is recognised throughout this book for its significant role in the creation of the district nursing movement.

As the oldest professional nursing organisation in the United Kingdom, the Queen's Nursing Institute has served as a model for other similar bodies around the world. Founded in 1887 with money collected for the Golden Jubilee of Queen Victoria, the charity was incorporated by Royal Charter and guided in its early years by eminent Victorians, led by William Rathbone and Florence Nightingale. Rathbone had employed the first district nurse back in 1859 and I am therefore conscious that I write with the weight of a long and very proud history behind me.

The national district nursing service that the Queen's Nursing Institute created brought skilled nursing care to people in their own homes for the first time. The Queen's Nurses who trained under its auspices were soon to be found throughout the country – from the largest cities to the smallest villages. Queen's Nurses were often trained as midwives and also as health visitors, so they came to know every member of the family, at key stages of the life course. Then as now, they also supported those who cared for other family members in need, through age or illness. Thus, when the National Health Service came into being in 1948, it inherited an established system of outstanding home and community nursing that had been built up over the course of several decades, through the vision and hard work of many individuals.

Today, the Queen's Nursing Institute continues to support all community nurses with professional development, learning and leadership opportunities. In 2007, the title of Queen's Nurse was reintroduced and there are now over 1200 Queen's Nurses working throughout England, Wales and Northern Ireland, leading by example and promoting the highest standards of patient care in the communities they serve.

Dr Crystal Oldman CBE
Chief Executive, The Queen's Nursing Institute

CHAPTER 1

HOW IT ALL BEGAN

'Of all the forms that charity takes, there is hardly one that is so directly successful as district nursing. It is almost true to say that wherever a nurse enters, the standard of life is raised.'
Charles Booth, *Life and Labour of the People of London. Final volume.*, p.157

IN THE POPULAR memory, the district nurse has always been a part of the community, but when did district nursing really begin? History tells us that sick men, women and children have been cared for at home since time immemorial, but it was not until the late 1800s that the professional, properly trained district nurse became a familiar figure in town and country. These were times when infant mortality was high, when life expectancy was short, medical knowledge was unscientific and Florence Nightingale had yet to pioneer professional training for nurses.

Charles Booth was a contemporary of William Rathbone VI. The final volume Poverty Series contains information gathered from the School Board visitors about living conditions and levels of poverty among the families for which they were responsible.
Courtesy of the Wellcome Library, London.

At the turn of the nineteenth century, the best that poor folk could expect was haphazard attention. On the one hand, there were well-meaning but untrained relatives, friends and neighbours who ministered to them as best they could, whilst for others the Poor Law or local charity was their only hope of help. Many parishes employed so-called nurses who visited the sick poor at home, but they were untrained and, like Nurse Philpot, who was engaged by the Poor Law Guardians of St Peter and St Paul, Bath, had negligible skills.

According to the records she dispensed senna and salts and was allowed money for the foul-tasting concoction of brimstone and treacle. She was also paid for staying with a woman who had smallpox. Nearby, another 'nurse' gave vaccinations, but there was no sense as to what was really expected of these women. Charles Dickens is well renowned for his characterisation of the Victorian nurse in his 1844 novel, *Martin Chuzzlewit*, with the infamous Sairey Gamp, described as a 'drink-sodden handywoman'. She, like her hospital counterpart, Betsey Prig,

Watercolour of an early district nurse in her outdoor uniform.
Courtesy of the Wellcome Library, London.

OUR NURSES.

Experienced Night Nurse (sternly). "COME, COME, SIR! YOU MUST STOP THAT HORRID NOISE. IF YOU KEEP WHEEZING AND SNORING LIKE THAT ALL NIGHT, HOW AM I TO GET TO SLEEP!!"

This cartoon 'Our Nurses' was first published in *Punch*, vol 61, p.225, 1871. *Courtesy of the Wellcome Library, London.*

had no training, and both were little more than domestic servants.

As to the charities, the religious element was clear. Healing and preaching were linked to the Gospels, so it followed that home visits to the poor were an opportunity for spiritual and moral uplifting. Amongst them were St John's House Nursing Institution in London, a religious community founded in 1848, whose aim was to 'train nurses for hospitals, families and the poor' and along the way raise the character of nurses and patients by providing moral and religious instruction. In London, two deaconesses belonging to the Mildmay Mission risked life and limb to care for the sick and their dependants in the slums of the East End in the late 1860s. There was also the Institution of Nursing Sisters,(originally called the Society of Protestant Sisters of Charity), founded by Mrs Fry in London in 1840.

Their aim was to provide 'experienced, conscientious and Christian nurses for the sick poor', with the intention of 'attending the poor in their houses'. It is very questionable just how much nursing their limited skills and training enabled them to give, but what they were expected to do was to teach the poor 'how to stop bleeding from a leech bite, how to dress a blister, how to make poultices etc'. More than anything, they were expected to show the poor how to help themselves, a sentiment that was to be stressed repeatedly in the ensuing years.

This illustration of Sairey Gamp
and Betsey Prig, appeared in *Martin
Chuzzlewit*. Mrs Gamp was a monthly
nurse and midwife, who would request
her clients to 'leave the bottle on the
chimley-piece and let me put my lips to
it when I am so dispoged.'
Courtesy of the Wellcome Library, London.

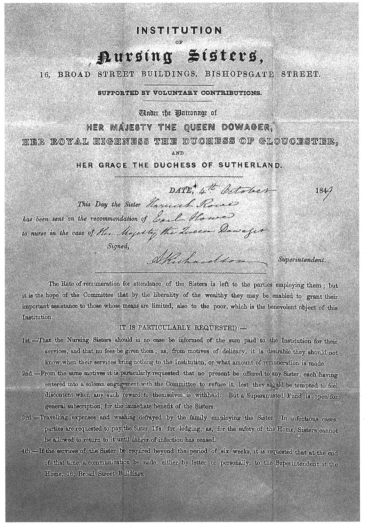

The Institution of Nursing Sisters, June 1849.
Courtesy of the Wellcome Library, London.

The two people responsible for permanently changing the face of home nursing care were Florence Nightingale (1820-1910) and William Rathbone VI (1819 – 1902)). Nightingale introduced the first professional training school for nurses in 1860, and Rathbone was inspired by his own personal family tragedy to set up a home-nursing experiment amongst the sick poor. Both were pioneering in their own way, but their collaboration was to change the face of health care for the poor for ever.

It was serendipity that just as Florence Nightingale was setting up her nurses' training school at St Thomas's Hospital, London, in 1859, many miles away in Liverpool, William Rathbone VI, a philanthropist, successful merchant and shipowner, and social and welfare reformer,

INSTITUTION OF NURSING SISTERS,

4. DEVONSHIRE SQUARE, BISHOPSGATE, N.E.

Under the Patronage of

HER LATE MAJESTY THE QUEEN DOWAGER,

HER ROYAL HIGHNESS THE DUCHESS OF GLOUCESTER,

AND

HER GRACE THE DUCHESS OF SUTHERLAND.

DATE, *14 Jan*   186 *4*

This day the Sister *Palmer*

has been sent on the recommendation of

to nurse in the case of *Mrs Jones*

Signed *S. Sweet* Lady Superintendent.

The Committee consider £1. 1s. per week to be a suitable charge for the attendance of the Sisters, but trust by the further liberality of the wealthy, they may be enabled to grant their important assistance to those whose means are limited, also to the poor, which is the benevolent object of this Institution. Applications must be made to the Committee for all cases of Consideration, previous to engaging a Nurse.

IT IS PARTICULARLY REQUESTED :

1st.—That the Nursing Sisters should in no case be informed of the sum paid to the Institution for their services, and that no fees be given them : as from motives of delicacy, it is desirable they should not know when their services bring nothing to the Institution, or what amount of remuneration is made.

2nd.—From the same motives it is particularly requested that no present, except a book of small value, be offered to any Sister, each having entered into a solemn engagement with the Committee to refuse it, lest they should be tempted to feel discontent when any such reward to themselves is withheld. But a Superannuated Fund is open for general subscriptions and donations for the benefit of Sisters who are past work.

3rd.—Sisters accepting Legacies from Patients, are ineligible for this fund.

4th.—Travelling expenses and washing defrayed by the family employing the Sister. In infectious cases, parties are requested to pay the Sister 15s. for lodging, as, for the safety of the Home, Sisters cannot be allowed to return to it until danger of infection has ceased.

5th.—If the Services of the Sister be required beyond the period of six weeks, it is requested that at the end of that time, a communication be made, either by letter or personally, and the remuneration forwarded to the Superintendent, at the Home, 4, Devonshire Square.

Superintendent's Report, The Institution of Nursing Sisters, which started out as the Society of Protestant Sisters of Charity, was established by Elizabeth Fry in 1840, and was one of the early attempts at reforming nursing in Britain. 11 June 1864. *Courtesy of the Wellcome Library, London.*

The Nightingale Home and Training School for Nurses opened its doors to trainees in July 1860, as part of the newly built St Thomas's Hospital, London. *Courtesy of the Wellcome Library, London.*

William Rathbone VI, who inaugurated the idea of employing trained nurses to attend the sick poor in their own homes, was a Liberal MP, a successful merchant and ship owner, as well as a social and welfare reformer.

was mourning the loss of his first wife, Lucretia. She had succumbed to consumption and during her dying days William had employed a private trained nurse, Mrs Mary Robinson, to provide her with the additional comfort of skilled nursing care. He later reflected on the plight of the poor, whose homes lacked even the most basic of comforts, and wondered how they coped in such circumstances. His answer was to set up an experiment in his home city whereby he re-engaged Mrs Robinson for three months, and sent her into one of the poorest

Florence Nightingale. William Rathbone relied heavily upon her opinion, and wrote of how submitted all his plans to her 'as we went along'. c.1895.
Courtesy of the Wellcome Library, London.

A typical Liverpool slum court, c.1900. The inhabitants of such deprived homes were exactly the people William Rathbone wanted benefit from the new district nursing service established in the city. c. 1905.
Courtesy of Liverpool Record Office.

districts of Liverpool to try, in nursing the poor, to relieve suffering and to teach them the rules of health and hygiene.

He recorded how he:

> '… furnished her with the medical comforts necessary, but after a month's experience she came to me crying and said that she could not bear any longer the misery she saw. I asked her to continue the work until the end of her engagement with me … and at the end of that time, she came back saying that the amount of misery she could relieve was so satisfactory that nothing would induce her to go back to private nursing, if I were willing to continue the work.'

William Rathbone certainly was willing and kept her in employment, but he realized that if the experiment was to work he needed more women like Mrs Robinson. But where, he asked,

Liverpool district nurse No. 29 on a round of one of her courts. c.1905.
Courtesy of Liverpool Record Office.

were they to come from? He turned to Miss Nightingale for advice for, as he said, 'In any matter of nursing Miss Nightingale is my Pope and I believe in her infallibility'. When the two began to discuss the idea, Florence Nightingale recognised that only the very best women could be selected because, unlike hospital nurses, they had to be able to work unsupervised most of the time.

Liverpool Nurse Training School and Home, 1865.
Courtesy of the Wellcome Library, London.

Her response was that he 'ought to train our own nurses in our own hospital, the Royal Infirmary', and this led to an arrangement whereby the Nightingale Fund agreed to open a nurse training school for hospital and district nurses in Liverpool. In return William Rathbone agreed to pay for the construction of a

ORGANIZATION OF NURSING.

AN ACCOUNT OF THE
LIVERPOOL NURSES' TRAINING SCHOOL,
ITS FOUNDATION, PROGRESS, AND OPERATION
IN HOSPITAL, DISTRICT, AND PRIVATE NURSING.

BY

A MEMBER OF THE COMMITTEE OF THE HOME & TRAINING SCHOOL.

WITH

AN INTRODUCTION, AND NOTES,

BY

FLORENCE NIGHTINGALE.

LIVERPOOL:
A. HOLDEN, 48, CHURCH STREET.
LONDON:
LONGMAN, GREEN, READER, AND DYER.
1865.

The Organization of Nursing describes how nursing should be carried out for a civilian population, and is an account written about the Liverpool Nurses' Training School and its foundation and development.
Courtesy of the Science Museum, London. Wellcome Images.

Florence Nightingale's *Notes on Nursing, What it is and What it is Not*, **a seventy-six page volume with three page appendix, was first published in England in 1859. In Nightingale's words, they were meant 'simply to give hints for thought to women who have personal charge of the health of others'.**
Courtesy of the Science Museum, London. Wellcome Images.

training school and nurses' home on land adjoining the Liverpool Royal Infirmary.

The training school opened in 1862, with Miss Mary Merryweather appointed Lady Superintendent. She had nursing experience from King's College Hospital and the pre-Nightingale Fund St Thomas's Hospital, and was given responsibility for recruiting and training suitable women. However, in the early years, she had difficulty retaining probationers, and although provision was made for thirty-one students, only seventeen were recruited in the first year.

Fortunately, things slowly improved and by the time Miss Merryweather left Liverpool to return to London in 1874, there were eighteen trained nurses serving in the newly-established districts, so providing the nurses with a new name of 'district nurse'. These districts had been created across the city, and each had its own committee and lady superintendent, a role which provided local ladies of good standing, including William's sister and his sister-in-law, with an outlet for their philanthropy. The women did not need any nursing experience but they had to be good administrators, for they were responsible for financing the costs of the nurses' board and lodging, for collecting and distributing medical comforts and making sure that case registers were kept. From time to time, they were also required to go on home visits, and even

A street group on district No. 3, circa 1905. *Courtesy of Liverpool Record Office.*

William undertook this task. For almost a year he acted as superintendent himself, making weekly visits with the nurse, overlooking the accounts and so forth. The sad fact was that the best that could be done for the poor and destitute people who were living in abject poverty in Liverpool's courts and cellars, with many families sharing one house in dirt and degradation, was to relieve hunger and provide shelter.

The responsibility of the lady superintendent changed in 1876 when each district was placed under the supervision of a district matron, whose job was to take charge of the nurse's professional work, leaving the lady superintendents to deal with the 'social and reform aspect'. Meanwhile, William Rathbone kept up a regular correspondence with Miss Nightingale, and in spring 1875, he sent her some statistical tables compiled from the nurses' case registers. Miss Nightingale was very impressed, describing it as:

Liverpool slum girls, circa 1905. *Courtesy of Liverpool Record Office.*

'... the most important document I have seen at all relating to the subject of district nursing ... it's revelations are extraordinary: and by me quite unexpected ... showing

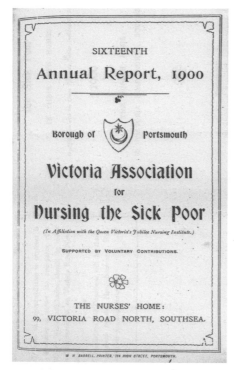

Title page of the 1896 *Annual Report of the Borough of Portsmouth Association for Nursing the Sick Poor*. The association was established in 1884, and became affiliated with the QVJIN in November 1892.

1. The extreme severity of the cases nursed by the district nurses. 2. The inevitable consequence of this viz: that you might employ ten times the number of nurses – really to nurse – and that the cases would find almost more than that with full nursing occupation. Your printed sheet shows... enough to do to employ fully a large staff of hospital trained nurses to nurse (and alone to nurse) in districts – a larger staff than we had any conception of. Only think what the cases must be when after weeding them into hospital and workhouses the death rate is 153 per 1,000!'

Nurse training was progressing well in Liverpool, and most importantly for this story, it introduced the idea that a district nurse needed to be a trained hospital nurse, preferably under the reformed Nightingale system. William's idea of district nursing was being taken up in other northern industrial cities. The Sick Poor and Private Nursing Institute was set up in Manchester and Salford in1864, followed by the Royal Derby and Derbyshire Nursing and Sanitary Association in 1865, the Leicester District Nursing Association between 1866 and 1867 and associations in York and Birmingham in 1870.

The front cover of the *Ranyard Magazine*, February 1917. This was more a news sheet, devoted mainly to religious matters.

Glasgow became the pioneering location of district nursing in Scotland in 1875 when Mary Oriell Higginbotham established the Glasgow Sick Poor and Private Nursing Association. Her objective was to provide free trained nursing care for those in need, as well as food, medicine, bedding, clothes and surgical appliances, and for these services also to be available to those who could pay. Yet another philanthropic woman, Lady Anne Lee Plunkett, the wife of the Archbishop of Dublin, set up St Patrick's Nurses' Home and Bible Woman Association in Dublin the following year, with a clear evangelical mission coupled with providing 'all such work as may be required for the patient.'

Alongside these pioneering organisations, a rather different pattern of district nursing was evolving in London. In 1874, the English branch of the Order of St John decided to start a scheme of district nursing, and looked to William Rathbone for advice. The outcome was the establishment of the National Association for Providing Trained Nurses for the Sick Poor, with Rathbone appointed chairman of the investigative sub-committee. When the sub-committee published their report in June 1875, it showed that provision of nursing care for the sick poor in and around the metropolis was very limited, and relied mostly on the services of the Ranyard Mission's bible-women nurses and the East London Nursing Society, both of which had been founded in 1868.

The former were supervised by lady volunteers, and carried out duties which blended preventive work and patching up with religious proselytizing. They referred patients to doctors and local hospitals, inspected infants in mothers' meetings and encouraged medical self-help among the poor. Mrs Ranyard was very much aware of the degree to which the poor looked after one another in emergencies and hoped to extend and improve these traditions with nursing assistance and advice. The East London Nursing Society had no religious aims, but set out to 'provide trained nurses to nurse Sick Poor in their own homes in East London' and initially engaged three private nurses to work in Bromley, Poplar and St. Philips, Stepney Way. After the Metropolitan and National Association for Providing Trained Nurses for the Sick Poor (MMNA) was established by Florence Lees, a St Thomas's trained nurse herself, in 1875, the East London Nursing Society joined forces with them, regained their independence in 1881, but later re-affiliated. Renamed the Metropolitan and National Association, the organization had a mission, which was to 'organize a system

Florence Lees (1840-1922) married the Rev Dacre Craven in 1879. In 1889 her book, *Guide to District Nurses and Home Nursing,* published in 1889, became the district nurses' bible for many years. She was awarded the Jubilee Medal and the Cross of St John of Jerusalem and remained, together with her husband, closely associated with district nursing until they retired to Essex in 1918. *Courtesy of the Wellcome Library, London.*

of training and supplying district nurses for the whole country' and an important provision was that the district nurses and the probationers should be suitably housed in nurses homes,

District nurse Jenny Wolfe, in her donkey cart at Gotherington, circa 1890s.

supervised by a highly trained nurse. They opened their Central Home and Training School at 23, Bloomsbury Square, London, and appointed Miss Lees as Superintendent-General.

The pioneers of Bloomsbury Square had to confront the most awful conditions, and on one occasion Miss Lees was called to a miserable 'home' consisting of a single room, where she found 'a child lying dead from scarlet fever on the window sill, the little sufferer having asked to be carried there; another child lying dead in bed; and a third suffering from the same disease, lying beside her'. On the other hand, the nurses themselves were frowned upon, and more, by the 'auld lichts of the "profession"' whom they disliked for the warnings they dispensed, invoking folk to 'keep their room clean and open their winder, clear out the things from under your bed …you'll feel just as if you were in a horspital'. The establishment were none too keen either, for in 1876, *The Lancet* launched an attack on Florence Lee's vision of district nursing as

This postcard of a Queen's rural district nurse on her village rounds was published in 1926 and is from a number produced in memory of Queen Alexandra. The cards were sold to raise funds for the Institute.

a profession for educated ladies, claiming that 'such work is better entrusted to strong, properly trained women of the lower class who have been accustomed to dirty work from their youth up'. Angry, Florence replied, 'The poor never seem to have any idea we are ladies.' Their class was not the point, but their skills as nurses was.

Another important district nursing initiative was underway in the small village of

Gotherington in rural Gloucestershire, where, in 1884, Mrs Elizabeth Malleson (1828-1916) set up a small experimental charity, the Village Nursing Association, to provide much needed village nurse-midwives. Enough money was raised to enable her to engage Nurse Mary, a 'trained' midwife and sick nurse in September 1885, and within weeks, the nurse had made 'ninety-six visits to invalids on her list', as well as attending midwifery cases. Nine months later, the experiment came to a halt when the money ran out. Whilst Elizabeth Malleson persisted with her efforts to provide village nurse-midwives, this time on a national scale, there were other local initiatives struggling to survive. In Cheltenham, the Reverend Fenn, the vicar of Christ Church, had provided a district nurse for the sick poor as early as 1867 and in Charlton Kings a parish nurse had been engaged in 1883 but, again, insufficient monies caused the scheme to be abandoned by Easter 1885. Nationally, small, independent rural nursing schemes had been successfully set up by philanthropic individuals, but they were scattered all over England. Elizabeth Malleson realised how much more could be accomplished by co-operation, and she envisaged a national association controlled by 'a central body which could set and maintain the standard of nursing, and which could ask for funds to help poor districts and to train suitable women'. She hoped to get the support of Florence Nightingale, and in June 1888, she wrote and asked that 'you may allow your honoured name to be placed at the head of the Association I hope to form'. Miss Nightingale declined the invitation for two reasons. She did not consider that Elizabeth's plans were detailed enough and she also doubted her credentials for setting up and running a national nursing association. Nevertheless, but she did send her 'valuable notes' for her 'encouragement and guidance'. Undeterred, Elizabeth persevered with her plan, but encountered opposition from many other quarters, including the medical profession, country residents whose deeply-rooted conviction was that things were quite all right as they were, having survived countless generations, and from the villagers themselves who were shy of any change. Sheer determination, persuasion and argument eventually paid off, and in May 1890 the Rural Nursing Association received the royal seal of approval. By September 1892, the RNA had nurses working in seventy-seven districts across twenty-five counties, and was soon to become a formal part of the newly created Queen Victoria Jubilee Institute for Nurses, as the QVJIN's Rural Nursing Branch.

CHAPTER 2

THE EARLY YEARS

BY THE TIME Queen Victoria celebrated her Golden Jubilee in 1887, district nursing had been elevated to a new status, and the practice was spreading across the country. As much as the widowed Queen wanted to celebrate her Jubilee quietly, the women of England were determined to honour the monarch in their own way, and through various committees, the Women's Jubilee Offering raised a vast amount of money. Even after the purchase of a specially commissioned necklace and earrings, there was a surplus of £70,000, and after much consideration, the Queen decided this money should be used for the welfare of nursing and nursing establishments. An advisory committee was set up, but *The Times* wasted no time in reaching their own conclusion, deciding that the money was intended to provide for the nursing of 'sick women and girls'. Apart from the raft of correspondence that this pronouncement precipitated from various quarters, William Rathbone and Florence Nightingale found

Queen Victoria established a tradition of inviting nurses to Buckingham Palace, which continued in subsequent reigns, 1901.

Queen Victoria's Jubilee procession through London.

VICTORIA OUR QUEEN.

themselves vying with several other organizations who each considered their nursing scheme to be the most appropriate beneficiary. These varied from a national pension fund for nurses to a holiday home for them, but ultimately, William Rathbone's plan, approved by Florence Nightingale, won the day. On 7 January 1888, *The Times* provided the public with the trustees' outlines of the scheme which provided for 'the foundation of an institution for promoting the education and maintenance of nurses for the sick poor in their own houses'. It was proposed that:

> '... the institution should have its chief centre in London but similar central institutions should be in Edinburgh and Dublin, and that with one, or all of them should be affiliated and institution desiring such affiliation, and satisfactorily fulfilling, in any part of the kingdom, the general purpose of the foundation. We would recommend that the nurses should all be duly approved women of excellent personal character, and of good education, similar to that of well-trained nurses in hospitals, and a special training in district nursing and maternity hospitals, so that they may be fit to attend poor women after childbirth.'

In July 1888, a year after her Jubilee, the Queen gave Rathbone's scheme her seal of approval and on 20 September 1889 she issued a Royal Charter, so establishing the QVJIN. The Queen became the first patron, cementing a tradition that has continued ever since, with enrolled nurses regularly being invited to meet their royal patrons at venues including Windsor Castle, Buckingham Palace, St James's Palace and Holyrood House, Scotland. She was exceptionally proud of her nurses and in 1896 invited all 539 on the Queen's Roll to visit Windsor Castle. Nearly 400 of them accepted, and the women, decked out in their uniforms, were transported by special train from London. Mary Stocks described how:

> 'Lunch was provided in a marquee ... at 5 o'clock they were assembled in the Park for inspection by the Queen, who, in her speech said, "I am very pleased to see my nurses here today, to hear of the good work you are doing and I am sure will continue to do."'

The ability of the institute to carry out this mission owed much to the Queen's generosity, for when she celebrated her Diamond Jubilee in 1897 a further royal endowment of £84,000 was made to the QVJIN.

Raising the standard of district nursing to meet the needs of a rapidly changing society was undoubtedly due to William Rathbone's skill, tact and determination, helped by Florence Nightingale and Florence Lees, who was responsible for elevating the status of the district nurse to a professional status.

William continued his involvement as honorary secretary of the Provisional Council, and in writing his *Sketch of the History and Progress of District Nursing* in 1890 was able to report:

> 'In Edinburgh, a most efficient Central Institution has been formed, on the best principles and with the highest standard of qualifications, and is in active operation, and there can be little doubt that, worked with the energy devoted to it, and the administrative talent for which the Scotch (sic) are so remarkable, its influence and example will extend

Two District (Queen's) Nurses are shown leaving the headquarters of the QVJIN on Castle Terrace, Edinburgh wearing cloaks and carrying their nursing cases. c.1910.
Courtesy of the Royal College of Nursing.

over Scotland a most valuable and complete system of nursing the sick poor in their own homes.'

A Central Training Home was established in the city, initially in a small flat in North Charlotte Street, but as demand grew, the home was soon expanded and was then moved to the splendid premises of Castle Terrace in 1890. With the energetic Miss Christian Guthrie Wright as honorary secretary, during the first year the Edinburgh QNs paid 7,517 visits to 321 cases, and a nursing association was set up in Dundee. Mary Higginbotham's Glasgow association amended its rules in 1889 and became affiliated to the QVJIN, and soon had a nurses' home and fourteen nurses in training.

The establishment of the Scottish branch of the QVJIN was a major factor in a slow improvement in the standard of nursing care in the Highlands and Islands and by 1900, 32 of the 225 fully trained QNs across Scotland were employed in these remote regions. The Lewis Hospital announced the appointed of its first QN in 1898, and by 1912 there were twelve district nurses in Lewis. Despite this, there were still not enough nurses for the region, and provision remained inadequate and inefficient until the recommendations of the 1912 Dewar Commission were embodied in the Highland and Island (Medical Services) Act of 1913. Lord Lovat, a committee witness, realised the benefit of the district nurse

The sitting room at Castle Terrace, c.1895.
Courtesy of the QNI Scotland.

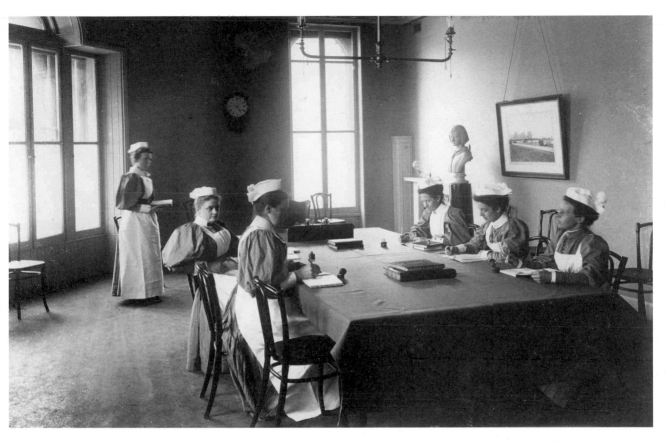

District nurses at Castle Terrace writing up their case books. c. 1895. *Courtesy of the QNI Scotland.*

Members of the Dewar Committee, 1912.

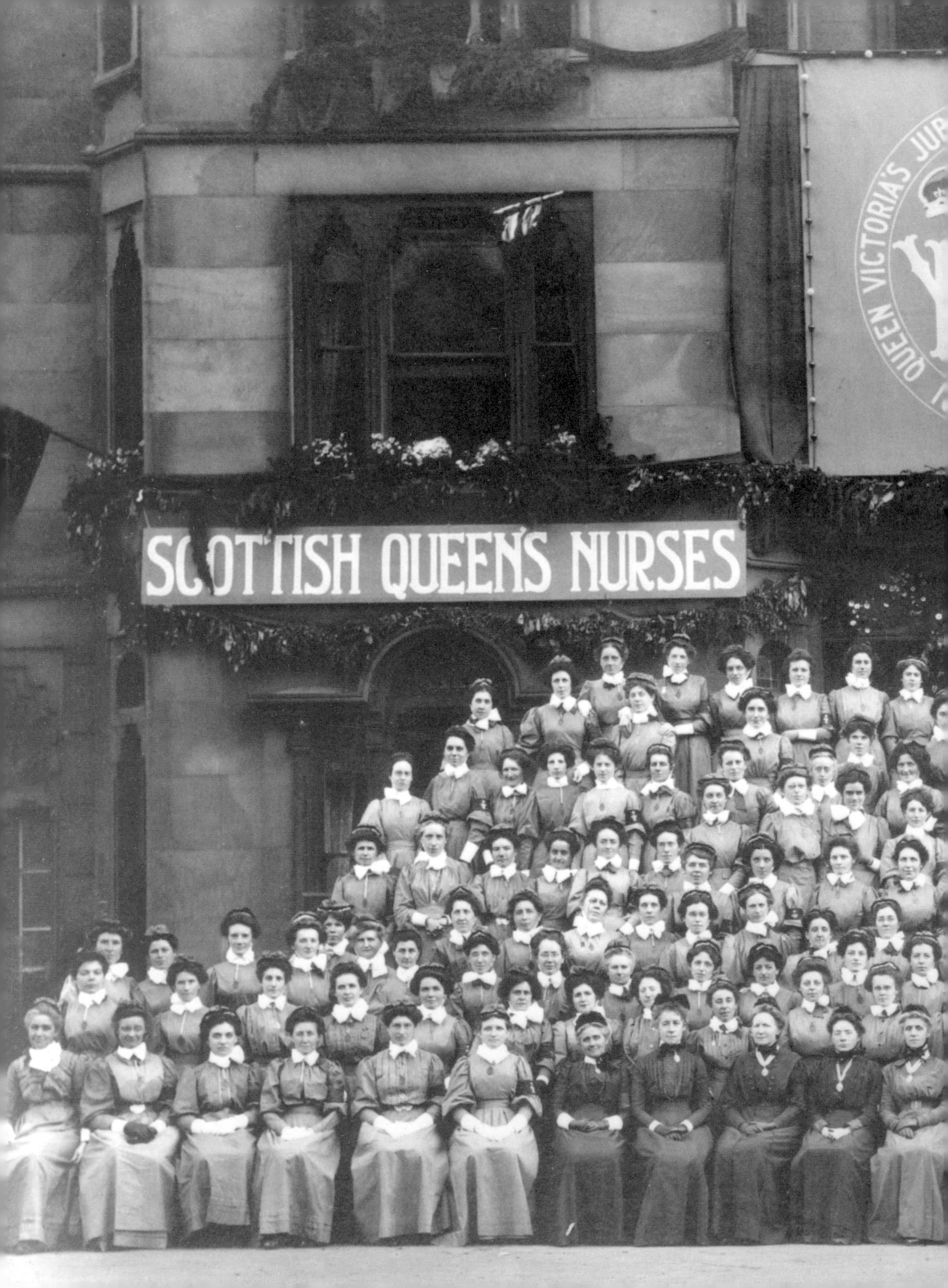
SCOTTISH QUEEN'S NURSES
QUEEN VICTORIA'S JU

QNs in Scotland, ready to meet their Majesties.
Courtesy of the Royal College of Nursing.

Queen Victoria being presented with flowers by a Victoria Jubilee Nurse at the Vice Regal Lodge, Dublin. c.1900.
Courtesy of the Wellcome Library, London.

when he stated, 'the medical salvation of the Highlands and Islands lies in organised nursing'.

Religious differences in Ireland made the initiation of district nursing schemes more complex, and resulted in two separate district nursing training homes being established in Dublin: St Patrick's for Protestant nurses and St Lawrence's for the Roman Catholics. Progress was made when a third was opened in Londonderry in 1904, for the two religious groups were taught in harmony with one another.

By 1902, Amy Hughes recorded that progress was being achieved, with QNs in every part of the country, even 'in the desolate island of Achill, where, to quote, "the people are nursed under conditions inconceivable except to those who have seen them. There is only one nurse to the eight thousand inhabitants, and Achill is twenty-five miles long and fifteen miles broad."' That the desperately poor isolated areas of Ireland had any nursing care at all was due largely to the pioneering work undertaken by Lady Dudley, wife of the Lord Lieutenant.

In 1903, she began a fundraising drive to provide a district nursing service for the poorest parts of the country, known as 'the congested areas', along the western seaboard. The link with the Lord Lieutenant ensured the nursing associations were seen as fashionable charities, with fundraising led by the old ascendancy families who held garden parties in aid of the Jubilee and Dudley nursing schemes.

The first Lady Dudley nurse to be appointed in Connemara was Elizabeth Cusack, who was sent to Belladangen in August 1903, followed by Catherine Wills to Carna some two months later. Neither post was for the faint-hearted; the very first edition of the *Queen's Nurses' Magazine* in 1904 described how Miss Wills had to 'walk two miles off the road through bogs to get to patients' cabins where she coped with maternity cases with the cow in the same room or where the tide came through the house'.

Wales had a linguistic rather than a religious problem, and when the Central Home was established in Cardiff, Welsh-speaking women had to be engaged to work in the rural areas, as so many of the older folk spoke no English. Eliza Jones was a school teacher before qualifying as a nurse in 1911 and as a QN in 1914, and not only did her application note that she was Welsh speaking, but also pointed out that she was not a cyclist. Quite how she got around her

Lady Dudley Fund district nurses visiting a patient's stone cottage in Ireland. *QNM, 31 December 1904.*

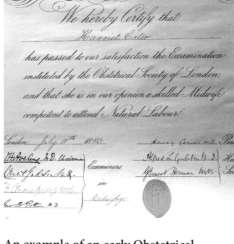

An example of an early Obstetrical Society of London certificate, 1883.

Miss Rosalind Paget was a niece of William Rathbone VI. *Courtesy of the Wellcome Library, London.*

district of Newton, Powys is a mystery, but she was a 'kind hard working nurse, interested and much liked' who, like all other women, had to resign when she married in 1919.

The new institute needed organizing, and so came under the jurisdiction of an executive council, whose first task was to appoint an Inspector General with responsibility for all nursing matters. The person they selected was Miss Rosalind Paget, who had an impressive background in nursing, having trained at the London Hospital and the London Lying-in Hospital, and had gained her Obstetrical Society of London diploma in 1885. Her appointment was innovative for it was the first time that a nurse had been put in charge of other nurses.

Before taking up the post, Miss Paget undertook the three month district training course at the Metropolitan and National Nursing Association in Bloomsbury, becoming the first QN. Her duties were far reaching, encompassing everything to do with the often thorny matter of affiliation, the training of nurses, setting up of schools for district nursing, and the granting of certificates and recommendations for enrolment.

Once conditions were worked out and sanctioned by the Queen, the way was open for local nursing associations to apply for affiliation if they chose. Liverpool DNA, and Manchester, established in 1864, were at the forefront of those that decided to apply to the Institute and by November 1891 thirty-one had been affiliated in England and Wales.

With the passing of the Midwives Act in England and Wales in 1902, district nurses who wanted to act as midwives had to pass the examination set by the Central Midwives Board. At this sitting in June 1906, there were 376 candidates, of whom 300 passed. On enquiry, only 190 of them said they intended to practice. *Nursing Notes,* July 1906, p.101.

Affiliation was by no means automatic, and the Ranyard Mission were rejected because not only was their training considered inadequate, but because religious proselytising was a fundamental part of their remit, a practice that was in direct conflict with the Institute's rules. Similarly, Menai Bridge were turned down because they insisted that their nurses be churchwomen. In contrast, Bristol, established in 1887, chose to remain an independent society until 1944. Others managed to become affiliated without complying with the prescribed conditions, including the East London Nursing Society whose twenty seven nurses did not live in district homes, and continued to be churchwomen. Some turned themselves down because they could not raise the funds needed and wanted a grant from the Institute, which they

District nurses leaving Liverpool Central Home for their morning round, c.1900. They started at 8.30 am and visited six to twelve patients before lunch. They went on duty again at five o'clock, revisiting patients to make them comfortable for the night. *Courtesy of Liverpool Record Office.*

could not afford. Others disaffiliated because their QN left and was replaced with a non-QN. There were also those who disliked the royal cipher and resented interference, whilst at times it was the local doctor who took against the arrival of the new style of nurse.

Until the introduction of the National Health Service in 1948, local associations had to cover all the costs relating to employing a district nurse, which included her wages, travel costs and accommodation, as well as the expense of essential items such as medicines, dressings and stationery. Raising money was a constant challenge and besides subscriptions, donations and midwifery fees, DNAs relied upon church collections and the efforts of local people who arranged fund-raising events. There were fêtes and flower shows, jumble sales and concerts, and, it seems, many football matches. Alford (Lincolnshire) Swifts Football Club held Boxing Day and Easter Monday matches, including a 'comic' match when half the team dressed as 'ladies' and played against the men, much to the amusement of the on-lookers, whilst

Miss Edith Pickering, an early QN.

in Portsmouth, in 1905, the ex-Mayor, Mr Pink, 'continued his good offices by handing over the sum of £32 1s 0d as part proceeds of a charity football match at Fratton Park'. However, the increases in the cost of living affected not only the nurses themselves but also those from whom subscriptions and donations were collected. The anomaly of rural district nursing lay in the fact that, in the areas where the nurses were most needed, the poor patients could least afford to subscribe towards the DNA funds. Despite the personal generosity and sterling fund-raising efforts of their committee members, many rural DNAs in Gloucestershire, especially those serving poor, often widespread communities, had difficulty raising adequate funds.

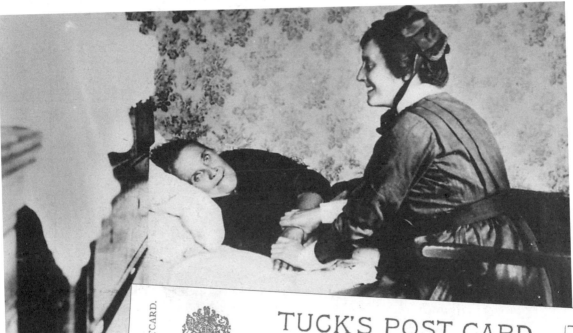

This postcard of an elderly patient and a Queen's nurse was published in 1926, and is from the collection produced in memory of Queen Alexandra, which were sold to raise money for the Institute.

POSTCARD.

Copyright London
Raphael Tuck & Sons' "REAL PHOTOGRAPH"
ART PUBLISHERS TO THEIR MAJESTIES THE KING & QUEEN.

By Appointment

TUCK'S POST CARD
CARTE POSTALE

THE NATIONAL MEMORIAL TO QUEEN ALEXANDRA.

Please keep the Ball rolling and help the Fund. Buy a Packet of these Cards (6 for 1/-) and send to friends. To be obtained from Local Nursing Associations or Queen Victoria's Jubilee Institute for Nurses, 58, Victoria St., S.W.1.

When the Portsmouth local corporation acquired the tramways in 1901 they rescinded the free travel offered to the district nurses by the previous private owner. The district nursing association found themselves with a bill of £12 12s 3d, an amount which almost doubled to £24 10s 2d. the following year, and continued to increase. Tram No 25, Clarence Pier terminus, c.1902.

Gotherington DNA reported a debit balance for many of the years between 1900 and 1915, and was rescued because Elizabeth Malleson, her husband, other family members and friends often covered the deficit by giving extra personal donations.

When Alford and District Nursing Association was set up in 1906, the organizing committee raised money through a subscription scheme which amassed £153 in the first year, but regardless of whether they had paid any money, no poor person was ever refused care.

The nurses themselves were never responsible for collecting money directly from patients, but were very often involved, with their superintendents, in fund-raising events. Besides a subscription scheme, local associations like the one in Portsmouth received money from a range of organisations including the army, the navy and the dockyard, from collecting cards and boxes, Friendly Societies, local churches, chapels and more. They also relied upon gifts of nursing appliances, old linen, clothes, books and magazines, and free

Henry Tate Badge.

Lady Ismay's husband inaugurated the Lady Margaret Ismay Badge in honour of his late wife, in 1901, the year she died. She had been president of the Birkenhead Society and a fund was established to pay for a QN to work for the Birkenhead District Nursing Society. During that time, the nurse could live in any of their Homes. The Lady Ismay badge had to be worn in addition to any other badges that the Birkenhead Society rules required.

Tate Nurse's Home.

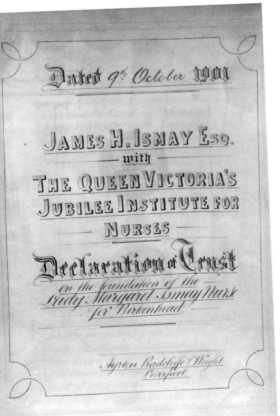

An early QN in the doorway of a cottage.
Courtesy of Peter Malczec.

Every QN was issued with a numbered bronze badge on enrolment, which was to be suspended on a light and dark blue cord. The silver and bronze badges were numbered on the reverse, with the number and date of issue recorded in the Roll of Nurses. On retirement, the badge had to be returned, and this was again noted in the Roll. The badges were then put back into circulation, so that any one badge might often be issued to several nurses.

The silver badge was worn by Queen's superintendents, and like the gold badge was to be suspended on a light and dark blue striped ribbon.

This gold badge was awarded in 1949 to Dorothy Jane Lewis for 21 years of service. She was appointed QN in 1926, then worked as a district nurse in Milford Haven and Colwyn Bay, where her Welsh came in very useful. She resigned in September 1948, aged 60.

tramway, omnibus and steamer passes for the nurses.

Legacies were an important source of support, and DNAs in Liverpool and London were just two who were to benefit. In 1902, Lady Tate, widow of the sugar magnate, Sir Henry Tate, made a gift of money to maintain the services of, and house a QN, for the Silvertown and North Woolwich DNA, and followed this with the Sir Henry Tate Memorial Home.

Later, Lady Tate provided funding for an additional QN for the Brixton DNA. The Tate Fund also provided emergency grants for QNs, and these were always recorded in the entry for a nurse in the Queen's Roll.

Keeping costs down was vital, and the *QNM* often included advise on how to make 'effective economies'. Chemists' bills could be reduced if, for example, the nurse only took very small quantities of medicines in her bag, and restocked twice a day if necessary. And she was advised that in 'ordinary chronic cases in poor districts, expensive dressings must be replaced by clean

Presentation of the long service medal, for 21 years of service. c.1910.

boiled rags and boracic fermentations'.

In the 1890s, the standard rate of pay for a QN in a rural area was between £25 and £30 a year, but she had also to be provided with her uniform at a cost of around £3 a year, and have her laundry and accommodation costs met. This might mean living in a cottage of her own, or it could be board and lodging in two furnished rooms, with attendance, fuel and light all included.

Nurses who were fit to be QNs had to look

QNs belonging to the Sussex County Association wearing brassards and badges with the 'VRI' monogram, 1906.

distinctive, and deciding on what would be fitting proved to be a long-winded process. It took the new uniform and badge sub-committee eighteen months, meeting monthly, to agree that there should be three classes of badge, made in bronze, silver and gold, each to be worn as a pendant around the neck.

To complement these, a brassard comprising the Queen's monogram, VRI, was to be worn on the left arm. The original design had the Queen's cipher surmounted by the imperial crown embroidered in gold on a four inch wide jubilee ribbon, but with hygiene in mind, it was decided to test it in disinfectant. One can almost see the look of horror on Lady Ponsonby's face when the colour turned yellow and the gold went black. The brassard was duly modified to dark blue dungaree material.

The matter of uniform was the source of similar lengthy debate, as it was clear from the outset that affiliated associations would ultimately have their own ideas on what their nurses should wear, driven largely by the cost. The Queen had the final decision, and she was presented with numerous different patterns from which to choose. The eventual choice was a floor length dress made of blue and white striped twill, with dark blue collar, cuffs and waistband, along with a white or dark blue apron, a plain, dark blue cloak, a cap 'frilled with lace or cambric', and to top it all, a bonnet made of black straw.

Uniform as illustrated in the *QNM* in 1913.

Tradition has it that the Queen 'improved' on the original bonnet presented to her by bending its brim into a Mary Queen of Scots peak, and so it stayed for many years to come. The new QNs were certainly a credit to their Queen, but at some considerable cost, for the whole ensemble was expensive, at £16 4s, which represented half a year's salary, or the equivalent of whole year's wage of a parlour maid. It was hoped that all QNs would wear the uniform but whether they did or not, they were required to wear the distinguishing badge and brassard whilst on duty. Changes in uniform included permission, in late 1905, for QNs to wear 'dark blue motor caps of an approved pattern instead of sailor hats when cycling or in country districts'. It seems that the design was not a success, for in January 1913, a prize of four shillings was offered to any QN who could come up with 'suggestions, with sketch or sample, of what in their opinion would be

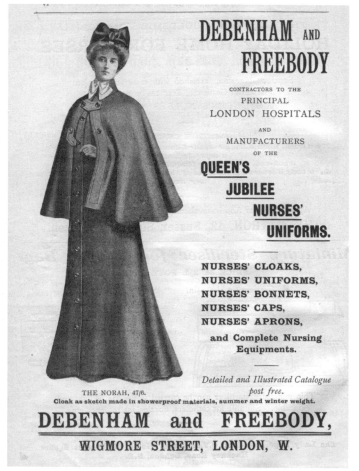

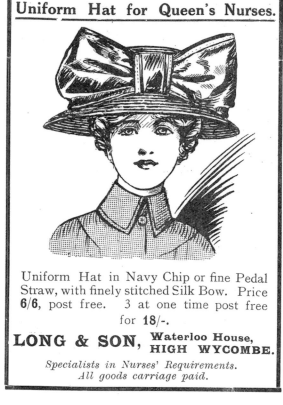

An advertisement from January 1913, showing the latest uniform hat.

This outdoor cloak was being advertised in 1905. The length of it was very unhygienic, but it was impossible to persuade nurses to have it made shorter.

a really comfortable and suitable cap for uniform wear in bad weather'. There was even a paper pattern supplied so district nurses could make up their own cycling knickers.

The scene was now set for the enrolment of the QNs, with Mrs Craven's manual, *A Guide to District Nurses,* by them at all times, acting as their bible. At the outset, before a nurse could embark on the six months' district training she had to have a minimum of one year's training in a recognised school attached to a general hospital. The hospital training requirement was gradually raised to three years by 1928, and in between, when state registration was introduced in 1919, already qualified QNs were encouraged to register, and eventually state registration became a pre-requisite for acceptance for Queen's training. Only single women could apply, and any nurse who chose to marry had to resign.

The district training itself was broad ranging and included subjects which the hospital-

40 | 40

ROLL OF QUEEN'S NURSES.

An entry from the Queen's Roll for Jane Poynton, who was appointed QN in 1893. She was forced to resign in 1896 after just three years for although she was good at her job, she did not get on well with the other nurses, and caused friction in the nurses' home.
Courtesy of the Wellcome Library, London.

trained nurse rarely encountered. QNs learnt about sanitation, plumbing, infection control and the importance of fresh air, they learned how to cook for convalescents, how to make blinds to shade windows and how to remove stains from toilets. This was in addition to learning how to nurse a wide range of medical conditions, often in the most adverse surroundings, where the ability to be adaptable and innovative were essential. At the end of the six-month training, the Queen's probationer sat an examination, and could refer to past papers which were regularly published in the *QNM* to help them prepare.

Those who were not going to work in big towns had to have three months' maternity training as well. Unlike their hospital counterparts, district nurses had privileged access to the homes of the poor, which gave them an unprecedented opportunity to educate their patients in matters of hygiene, health and diet, but what they did not do was give alms, nor were they allowed to bring religion into their visits.

Supervision was a fundamental part of life as a QN, and in towns was undertaken in the nurse's home by the Queen's appointed superintendent. It was her job to organise the daily round and allocate jobs, to check the nurse's work, case notes and district bag. The rural QN had no such overseer, and on a day to day basis was left to her own devices, but like her town counterpart, was subject to periodic inspection of their work by an inspector sent from headquarters, to ensure she was carrying out her duties properly. The reports made no distinction between

Queen Victoria's Jubilee Institute for Nurses.

EXAMINATION for the ROLL of QUEEN'S NURSES 19th June, 1924.

1.—How would you test whether the water from any particular tap comes from the main or from a cistern? Enumerate the different sources of supply of water to large towns. In the event of an epidemic attributed to a polluted water supply, what precautionary measures would you advise householders to adopt?

2.—What are adenoids? In what ways are they disadvantageous to the individual? What after-care is required by a school child who has had adenoids removed by operation?

3.—You are called in to a case of precipitate labour. How would you, as a district nurse, deal with this emergency? What are the dangers to be guarded against?

4.—Make out a sample page of your case-book and fill in the likely particulars of a 'bus-driver, aged 42, whom you have nursed through pneumonia, and who recovered.

5.—In nursing a case of Cancer in an advanced stage, with foul discharge, what method would you adopt for the comfort of the patient and the household?

6(a).—Give notes of a short "talk" to mothers on the importance of warmth for their infants.

or

6 (b).—What are the functions of an Infant Welfare Centre? Describe what premises are required, also how weighing is carried out and recorded.

Questions 6(a) and 6(b) are alternative; only one should be answered.

Three hours is allowed for the examination.

By 1924, the exam questions had become far more complex, a reflection of the advancement of medical knowledge.

An early school nurse in Liverpool.

on and off duty, and almost every one emphasised the main concern that a nurse should be neat, orderly and tactful, and her whole life an inspiration to orderly habits in the neighbourhood. Two reports from an inspection in Boxford in 1905 demonstrate this. The first commented:

'Work excellent, very neat capable nurse. Baskets beautifully neat and well fitted. Books in order. Nurse shares house with friend who sometimes takes a private case. They have no maid. Everything about the house and all the details most finished and neat …'

The second made no bones about the unsuitability of the nurse:

'Books not well kept, lives alone, house untidy. Is liked by patients … is inclined to give

Scottish district nurses getting ready to go out on their district rounds, c.1900.

a great deal of time to some and to neglect others. I have advised Miss Perceval not to keep her.'

The scope of the district nurses' work soon expanded to include school nursing, and provided a very valuable service. The Metropolitan and National Nursing Association first sent a QN into the Vere Street Board School in 1891, and before long:

'... a nurse visited the school every morning and spent between one and two hours seeing twenty-forty children and dealing with burns, cuts, abscesses, opthalmia etc. as well as examining for dirt and vermin.'

The manager, Mrs Leon, had no doubt that school attendance increased as the children had their sores taken care of, prevented much pain and discomfort and the spread of infectious diseases. Liverpool was not far behind, and in 1895 Mrs William Rathbone paid for a nurse to attend to the minor ailments of school children, and within nine months 1,000 children had been seen. In 1902, the Liverpool DNA took over responsibility for the nurse, and engaged an additional nurse, and when the Liverpool Congress met in 1909, Herbert Rathbone was able to report that there were four full time school nurses working from the nurse's home, as well as two QNs who attended school one day a week. One element of the 1907 Education Act was the introduction of the systematic medical inspection of elementary school-children, which, as the *British Journal of Nursing* discussed in August 1908:

Queen Alexandra receiving her QNs in the gardens of Marlborough House, where she presented them with their certificates and badges. 3 July 1901.

'... opened up a new field to the nursing profession, and it is certain that the service will require a type of nurse adequately trained and possessing in a marked degree the characteristics of tact and keen observation.'

In fact, those that applied came from all walks of life, and included the daughters of clergymen, sea captains, merchants, a coast guards officer, a stockbroker and even an Oxford professor.

In 1896, there were 539 QNs on the official roll, a number which increased to around 900 in 1900. Even though nearly 200 names were included in the Queen's Roll in 1900 itself, there would have been more if over 100 women had not left the service, either because they got married or because their health suffered from the hard physical nature of the work.

Queen Alexandra's speech.

It gives me great pleasure to receive you all here to day and it is most gratifying to me to be a[ble] to carry on the noble work founded by our dearly bel[oved] and never to be forgotten Queen Victoria.

I have always taken the most sincere interest [in] Nurses and Nursing and it affords me heartfelt satis[fac]-tion to be associated with you in your labours of l[ove] and Charity. I can indeed imagine no better or hol[ier] calling than that in which you are engaged of tending the poor and suffering in their own homes in the hour[s] of their greatest need.

I shall follow with interest the reports of the Institute and shall anxiously note the progress which you are making from year to year.

I pray that God's blessing may rest upon your devoted and unselfish work and that He will have you all in His Holy keeping.

Alexandra

Chapter 3

LIFE ON THE DISTRICT BEFORE 1914

WHEREVER THEY WORKED, in town or country, life was hard for the district nurse. The hours were long, as the new district nurse who arrived in Staverton, Gloucestershire in 1902 found out, for she was expected to:

> '… start upon her rounds every day at 9 o'clock and generally be in by 8 o'clock in the evening. Anyone who wishes to see her about small dressings, small accidents etc. should call by 8.30 in the morning, or 8 o'clock in the evening, when the nurse will generally be in. Of course, messages may be sent to Nurse, to go anywhere, at any time.'

The building of a local railway near Gotherington in 1905 brought many navvies and their families to the neighbourhood and in just one month during that year, Miss Margaret Powell recorded a huge workload of 'over eight hours a day for thirty consecutive days and four nights on duty'. Typhoid epidemics, which the hospitals would not deal with, were just such an emergency; in Wantage in 1906, there were ten cases of typhoid and one death in a row of cottages 'where the rooms were without windows and fireplaces and the only water a supply from a stream at the side of the road that was nearly dried up, the nurse was on duty day

This postcard, published in 1926, is from the collection produced in memory of Queen Alexandra, and shows a QN on a home visit to a mother and her new baby.

and night'. Home operations, considered to be less disruptive to family life, and were, in many cases, safer than being in hospital, involved the nurse in a great deal of preparation. She was expected to get the patient and the room ready for a surgical procedure and to help the doctor, which according to Miss Loane, giving advice in *Nursing Notes* in February 1898, included sweeping chimneys, disinfecting dustbins, getting rid of pets and preparing the kitchen table for the operation. To restore the patient afterwards she was exhorted to use 'smelling salts, three pennyworth of brandy, a fan, ice, strong coffee and a new laid egg'. Letters from QNs in 1909 give an idea of the variety of operations the nurse encountered, ranging from:

> 'ovariotomy (several) lithotrity, extra uterine, herniotomy, caesarean section, amputation of breast, fingers, toes (but no legs) glands, cysts, tracheotomy, and of course tonsils, adenoids and circumcisions any amount also several nephrotomies, appendicitis...'

The work which district nurses undertook in the Scottish Highlands and Islands was not only varied but was often hazardous. The QN on Stornoway, who, besides her district work, was in charge of the little hospital, aided by a trained nurse and probationer, had to deal with some unusual patients in late June 1904, when the Danish steamer, the *Norge*, sank off the Scottish coast with the loss of around 700 lives. Amongst the rescued emigrants, the nurse wrote of having 'twenty one cases in hospital, Norwegian Swedes and Russians, thirteen are

A carriage lent for a tubercular case, Liverpool, c.1900s. *Courtesy of Liverpool Record Office.*

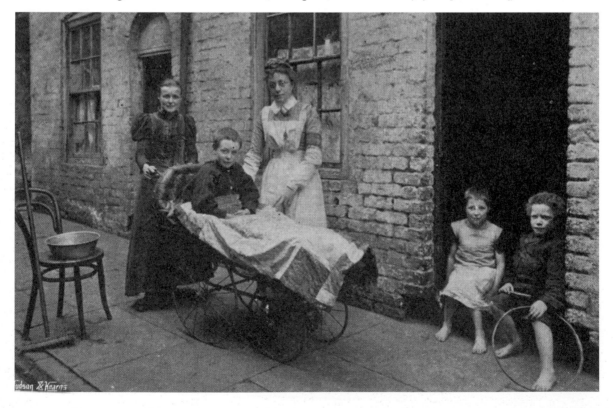

A district nurse in a remote area, possibly Yorkshire.

A district nurse visiting a family on Arranmore Island, Co. Donegal, Ireland. c. 1906-10.

QN Miss Hall, set up this revolving shelter, measuring 6ft by 7ft in a field adjoining her patient's cottage in June 1905, where he was treated, successfully, in the open air, for chronic pneumonia.

children of whom two died last night. They are all badly frost bitten'. Only fourteen of them survived. It is clear that having a district nurse on such a remote island had a great impact on the islanders, for after one joined the newly affiliated branch on Gigha, Argyllshire, in May 1911 the secretary wrote:

> 'As so often happens when medical help is required, stormy weather makes it well nigh impossible for the doctor to cross over, but since Nurse … came to the island there is a feeling of quiet security in the minds of the inhabitants, which is welcomed, as well as greatly appreciated by them.'

The school master on Fair Isle was equally complimentary about 'how well they were served by a most excellent nurse, which was just as well for according to the nurse, the doctor had only visited once in the past seven years'.

There were innovative treatments taking place as well, for Miss Hall, the QN in Penshurst,

A page from the *QNM* showing the various ways that Scottish district nurses got around their, often remote, districts.

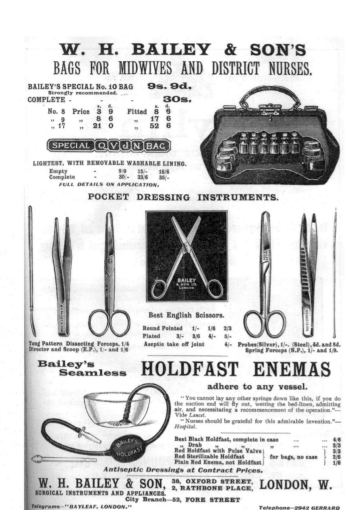

An advertisement for a district nurse's bag, 1909.

Kent, adopted and adapted the much-discussed sanatorium treatment for one of her patients who was suffering from chronic pneumonia and complications. By December 1905, she reported that he was much better. This was despite the cold weather, which did not surprise Dr William Paget-Tomlinson, writing in the *British Medical Journal*, who noted that patients did much better in the winter than in the summer.

For one district nurse in the West of Ireland in December 1904 'the hardest thing to contend with is superstition, combined with old customs as regards the sick', with another recording how she had been :

'attending a case of ulcerated leg for some days. I called unexpectedly one evening and found the patient had been treating her leg in an extraordinary manner. I discovered a large piece of moss, with earth attached to it, laced on the open sore, with the earthen side next it. I naturally felt quite irate and asked why my treatment had been abandoned. I received a long explanation of the virtues attached to the moss cure, and was told an old woman prescribed it … [S]uperstition was, of course, at the back of all this. I merely relate this as an instance of some of the difficulties a nurse has to meet in dealing with patients of this class.'

Another of Lady Dudley's nurses reported her experiences with a maternity case in 1910. She wrote:

'Had just gone to another case when this patient sent for me. Then they went for [the] handy woman, who is a great scold. Doctor also had to be sent for, and he would not have me go whilst this woman was there. Afterwards I was called. The house is an old stable. There is no bed in the house, just a table, one chair and one stool; they are very poor. Patient was lying in the corner in a frightful condition. I got assistance and had her removed and made her comfortable.'

Getting around the district was often arduous, especially in remote areas. In Gotherington, the nurse got around on a donkey, and in 1901, when she was joined by another nurse, an additional donkey and a bicycle were purchased for them. The donkey was not replaced with a hardier pony until 1910. Miss Reeve, working in Kent in 1905, also used a pony and cart, but in the winter when she had to visit a man with pneumonia who lived a mile off a driveable road, she had to abandon the cart and tramp across fields which were deep in mud. It was even worse for the district nurse on Lewis who was trying to get to a patient during a severe storm:

> 'I went out at 5 pm and although I had not a mile to walk, on my return it took me more than one hour to find my way back to the end of the street, there to discover more than eight feet of snow to cut through, and all in two and a half hours owing to the blizzard … the blizzard lasted for two days and nights.'

It was perfectly reasonable then for prospective rural district nurses to be asked on their application form 'Are you a good walker and accustomed to the country?'

Life was especially hard, and potentially lonely for district nurses working in rural areas, for besides being in remote, often inaccessible parts of the country, many of them were solely responsible for their patients, and had no easy access to a doctor.

In the 1890s, there was no standard rate of pay for rural areas, mainly because local circumstances

An Edwardian district nurse on her bicycle.

and arrangements varied so much. Buxton, a newly affiliated rural branch to which Miss Loane was appointed in 1893, was responsible, like all DNAs, for raising its own funds, including the nurse's salary at a suggested rate of between £25 and £30 a year for a QN. By 1909, the suggested wage of £30 a year had become a required minimum, independent of local conditions, rising to £32 and £35 in the second and third years of service, with an additional £2 a year for practising midwifery. This was at a time when a cook-housekeeper earned an average wage of £35 per annum in the provinces and £41 in London, whilst an upper-housemaid could earn £25 a year, all found.

The DNA also had to provide the district nurse's uniform at a cost of around £3 a year, cover laundry costs and accommodation, preferably in a cottage of her own, or board and lodging in two furnished rooms, with attendance, fuel and light. Often there was little to choose between the two options, but in any event the nurse had to live within the community she served. Many of the cottages were every bit as dilapidated as those of their patients, and lacked gas, electricity, running water or drains. Lucy, Countess St Aldwyn, and two other committee members of the Coln St Aldwyn DNA paid 'the cost of cottage furniture for the District Nurse' in 1911, but furniture and fittings often consisted of secondhand donations. Part of the annual inventory for the nurse's cottage at Upton St Leonards in 1908 reads '6 tea plates (odd ones), 5 teacups (odd), 6 saucers (odd)' and notes such as 'faded', 'worn out', 'broken' and 'of no use' are made in every room. Life for the QN who was billeted in lodgings was not always much better, for she often had to put up with an unsympathetic landlady who did not like the inconvenience of the odd hours the nurse was forced to keep. Words of wisdom from Miss Loane included advice that:

> 'the country nurse needs good boots, warm light underwear, stout umbrellas and the lightest possible district bag … she needs a good solid manly breakfast and should never leave home for a long round without a sandwich.'

In 1909, the district nurses' workload was increased by the introduction of public health work, which involved assisting with the medical inspection of schoolchildren, visiting cases of tuberculosis, health visiting and care of mentally-defective children.

Nurses standing outside the Queen's District Training Home, Essex County Training Home, in Leytonstone. c.1911.
Courtesy of the Wellcome Library, London.

Staff and patients at the Hammersmith Minor Ailments Centre, Hammersmith and Fulham DNA, *QNM*, July 1913.

Staff and patients at the Hammersmith Minor Ailments Centre, Hammersmith and Fulham DNA, *QNM*, July 1913.

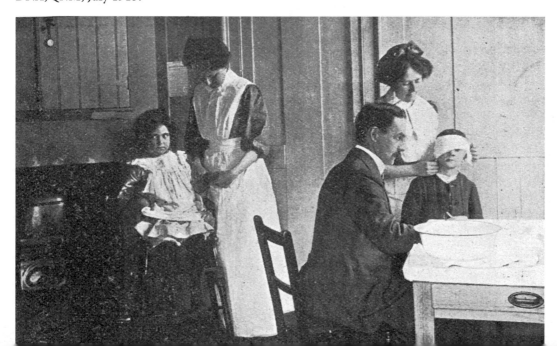

There was also the issue of how the nurse's services were to be paid for and different systems of payment evolved side by side, with provident schemes remaining popular. In 1898, Jamieson Hurry wrote *District Nursing on a Provident Basis* in which he suggested a subscription of 1s a year for an individual, or 2s 6d for a family. By this he calculated that a population of 4,000 would be able to support one nurse. He listed towns that already operated the system, including Daventry and Stockton-on-Tees and the counties of Gloucestershire, Dorset and Lincolnshire. At the time, the average wage of a working man was between twenty and thirty shillings a week, so the cost of employing a private nurse was completely beyond most families. The benefit of the provident system was that people would pay a small amount of money regularly to qualify for the services of a district nurse. A similar system was already in use for other services, for example the medical dispensaries and fire services, and was like paying insurance, except the nurses themselves were frequently required to collect fees from patients who could afford it. The introduction of the National Insurance Act in 1911 paved the way for the welfare state, but it did not allow for universal free health care, so the QVJIN continued to provide a nursing service financed as best it could from donations from the better off, subscriptions from patients willing to pay and soon payments from the state whenever they could get them.

A group of QNs at a garden party given in 1912 by the Duke of Devonshire at Devonshire House, attended by Queen Alexandra. The postcard is from the collection produced in memory of Queen Alexandra, published in 1926, and sold to raise funds for the Institute.

Chapter 4

QNs AT WAR, 1914-18

'Since the issue of the last *Queen's Nurses Magazine*, great and terrible events have come to pass. Three months ago little did we dream that the subject of our next editorial would be concerned with the work of QNs in time of war.'
QNM Editorial, October 1914

THE EDITORIAL WENT on to talk about how 'greater efforts and sacrifices may be demanded from each one of us before this crisis is at an end' and the author urged QNs to 'prove that we really do put country before selves'. In many cases, this meant staying at home and being 'content to go on in the usual routine, attending to their districts, with hardly time to wish that they could be spared for "active service"' and by so doing bore 'fully as noble a share in the nation's burden'. This sentiment was echoed by one Superintendent writing in October 1914:

'I have told my nurses that they can do as great a work as any woman for the nation at this time by teaching the people how to economise and by looking after the families of those who are fighting for their country.'

As the war progressed, so the shortage of district nurses at home became a matter of concern. In 1914, 2,096 QNs were at work, but by mid-1915 there were 400 of them away, prompting the nursing committee to consider whether the training rules might be relaxed. By late 1916, this number had increased to 652, whilst Scotland, which retained its own roll. had lost 147 of its 413 QNs to active service. This had an impact on the scope of work undertaken at home, but the remaining nurses were commended for giving 'ungrudgingly of their strength and services to ensure that the dependants of the men at the front, and the sick poor generally,

The new style uniform, was being advertised in the *QNM* in January 1914. 'The coat is cut to give more width across the chest; collar can be worn open or closed. The dress is made in the "coat frock" style with a loose belt.'

A district nurse on duty, attending patients in their homes, *QNM,* July 1915.

shall in no way suffer through lack of necessary nursing attention'.

It was also made clear that if QNs were granted leave of absence to take up war-related work, it was on the understanding that they would return later on 'to complete the term of service due under their agreements'. No DNA wanted to see their district nurse leave, but they understood their feelings of patriotism, and often gave generous parting gifts. When QN Miss Mary Sutton left her post in Carrick-on-Shannon, Co. Leitrim, Ireland for Bordeaux in November 1914, she was presented with 'a gold purse of sovereigns by her Committee and a few friends, as a small token of their appreciation for what she has done in the district'.

Regardless of where they were working, readers of the *QNM* were eager to know what QNs were doing for the war effort, and letters published throughout the years of conflict provided a unique insight into the experiences on the ground, in far off lands as well as on the home front.

As qualified nurses, many QNs were already signed up to the Queen Alexandra Military Nursing Service Corps Reserve (QAIMNS[R]), set up in 1908, or had joined the Territorial Force Nursing Service (TFNS) originally formed the same year to staff the territorial force hospitals at home, or had put their names on the Civil Hospital reserve.

As reservists, they continued to work in civilian posts and private homes in peacetime, but made an annual commitment to the War Office and were ready to be mobilized if war was declared. Initially, the TFNS members were restricted to undertaking their wartime service in the United Kingdom, not only in the twenty five territorial hospitals, but also in hundreds of auxiliary units throughout the British Isles. However, as demand for nurses abroad grew, they were given the opportunity of working abroad, and many were employed in the eighteen territorial hospitals on the Western and Eastern Fronts, and alongside their QAIMNS colleagues in military hospitals and casualty clearing stations in France, Belgium, Malta, Salonica, Gibralter, Egypt, Mesopotamia and East Africa. But there were also QNs who allied themselves to organisations abroad including the French Flag Nursing Corps, the Red Cross, the Society of Friends, the Urgency Cases Hospital, the Scottish Women's Hospital and the exotic sounding Prince Volansky's Flying Field Ambulance Service in Russian Poland.

Like their nursing counterparts, district nurses who were signed up to the TFNS received a standard letter calling them up for service, modified to include their personal name and destination. It advised them how to proceed:

Miss C. Wills and other QNs who were working for the Territorial Force Nursing Service (TFNS) at the First Eastern General Hospital, Cambridge. The Florence Nightingale designed scarlet cape, with the distinguishing 'T' badge on one corner, was worn during the day, and was designed to be long enough to 'conceal the female bosom from the gaze of the licentious soldiery.'

'Madam, you are requested to join your unit of the Territorial Force Nursing Service at once. A railway warrant is enclosed which entitles you to travel free and should be surrendered to the Booking Clerk in exchange for a 1st class ticket. A travelling claim is also enclosed. Will you kindly fill in both carefully, with the date, line and route by which you travel. On arrival you are to report yourself to the Administrative Medical Officer of the xxxxxxxxx Hospital, and also to your principal Matron, Miss xxxxx. The sum of £8 will be issued to you for your TFNS uniform, which you must obtain as soon as possible if you have not already done so, and in the meantime, wear your own uniform.'

Any idea of leisure time was quashed by the final sentence which advised nurses that 'it will not be necessary for you to have any plain clothes so you need not bring much luggage'.

Miss C.A. Tait McKay was one of the first QNs to describe working on the home front. She had superb credentials which included being a highly qualified nurse, a district nurse, county superintendent and inspector of midwives for Cornwall. She had joined the TFNS in 1911 as a Sister before being promoted to Matron in August 1912, and when she was called up on 11 August 1914, was appointed acting matron of the 520 bed 4th Southern General

Hospital, Plymouth. Here she had a staff of twenty-two sisters, two masseuses and sixty-eight staff nurses, seven of whom were QNs, and during her tenure had twelve QNs working under her command. The hospital was created by transforming the Salisbury Road Schools and the adjacent Baptist Church, and every class room had been converted into a ward with twelve to fifteen beds. Miss McKay told readers how four days after the staff took up their posts in August 1914:

> 'The first batch of 102 wounded warriors arrived from the front on 21 August, forty of those were stretcher cases. They came into Plymouth in an ambulance train which pulled into Friary Station at 5.30 pm and as soon as the news leaked out, considerable excitement prevailed. … a hot bath, some chicken broth and the kindly attentions of the nursing staff did much to revive their spirits.'

The second batch numbering in all 132, including fourteen Germans, arrived on 25 September. She later recalled how that the average number of beds was about 1,450 and how in the summer months 'huge extensions were added with tents and marquees, which usually came down in

A group of QAIMNS Reserve Force staff, made up of matrons, sisters and staff nurses under forty-five who could be called upon at short notice They had to sign a three year contract and received either an annual five pounds retaining fee or, if working, a scaled allowance.
Courtesy of Sue Light.

November'. She had the honour of being presented to the King and Queen when they visited the hospital on 9 September 1915.

Brighton Grammar School was another example of a requisitioned building which was converted for military use, becoming the 520 bed Second Eastern General Hospital. More than a quarter of the one hundred nurses were QNs, and were there ready to accept their first convoy of 300 wounded men when they arrived from Mons on September 1914.

By then it became evident that the existing military hospitals had insufficient accommodation to cope with the demand as casualties flooded into Britain. Extra beds had to be provided quickly and one solution was to build hutted wards in the grounds, which was what happened at the 955-bed Royal Victoria, Netley, one of the largest and most important hospitals. By the time that QN Ethel Nazer was posted in November 1914, twenty-five of the proposed forty-five huts had been built, accommodating 500 of an anticipated 800 patients. The ward huts, she wrote, were 'quite nice for temporary buildings; ten beds on each side with two closed –in coke stoves at top and bottom' but it was the patients themselves that were the biggest surprise. Many of them were Sikhs and Gurkhas, a novelty which:

'seemed so strange at first to have twenty dark turbaned faces gazing at one; even in bed they like their heads covered; some when they arrive have lost their puggarees and they will insist on using their towels until we are able to replace them from the stores.'

Between January 1915 and March 1919 the cloister of the Abbaye de Royaumont, near Asnières, just twenty-five miles behind the front line, served as a 100 bed hospital. Set up by the Scottish Women's Hospital, several QNs volunteered and worked there as part of the medical team, whilst the artist, Norah Neilson Gray (1882-1931) was a VAD nurse. *Courtesy of Argyll and Bute Library Service.*

Her description of their wounds mirrored those that many other nurses encountered, with:

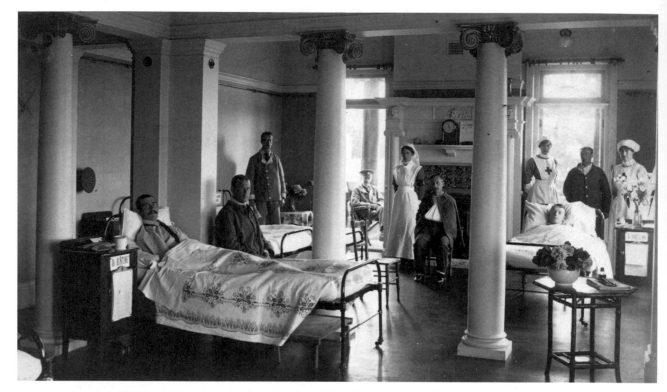

Battenhall Mount Red Cross Hospital, where Miss Murphy, Queen's Nursing County Superintendent for Worcester, and her staff, which included some of her district nurses, cared for the sixty one wounded soldiers being treated there. Four DN's were always amongst the day staff rota, and one worked alongside the other staff at night. *QNM,* June 1915.

'five out of the last twenty were hand and arm wounds and these walked in; the other fifteen were heavy stretcher cases; some had six and eight wounds from shrapnel and three were badly frost bitten; one has since died, another developed tetanus and several amputations have had to be done; all the wounds are horribly septic on arrival but it is surprising how quickly they clean up with regular dressing and attention.'

As for the facilities for the nurses:

'We sleep in tiny cubicles nine in each hut, our sitting room is a hut and so is our mess room and yet another is the bath-room hut containing two Geyser baths which have to duty for all the nursing staff, numbering at present seventy eight...'

Meanwhile, others continued their district work in the community, and an inspector writing in the *QNM* in January 1915 expressed the view that:

'the harder part is that borne by those who stuck to their posts, the monotonous daily rounds of 'chronics' and 'babies' with the few 'acutes' which are so important and are so often a source of anxiety on the district; work so well worth doing, but unknown and unrecognized save by the discerning few.'

Many hard-working district nurses devoted all their leisure to Red Cross work in various ways, willing and anxious as one wrote in October 1914, 'to do double duty so far (sic) we can without neglecting our patients'. District nurse, Miss M. Urquhart had a rather different job at a National Shell Filling Station where her new position was:

> 'Distinctly welfare work among the women and girls here, and the duties comprise the engaging of suitable overlookers; investigations of complaints of the workers; cases of the dismissal; keeping records of broken time; general supervision of working conditions during day and night and of canteens and rest rooms.'

> Her nursing skills were not forgotten for she was also 'in close co-operation with nurses and doctors regarding the physical well-being, cleanliness, clothing etc. of my 3,000 girls'.

In the early years of the war every district nurse was urged to:

> 'throw herself more entirely into her sphere, to make herself indispensable to the people by identifying herself with their joys and sorrows as well as their ills, and by so doing keep awake the diminishing sympathy of those good people who have for so long past been staunch friends to the district nurse and her work.'

It was no longer automatic that the district nurse attended a definite case of illness, for much of her work was taken up in other ways, all connected with public health. Their influence was such

This is a ward hut at Netley, where QN Ethel Nazer worked.

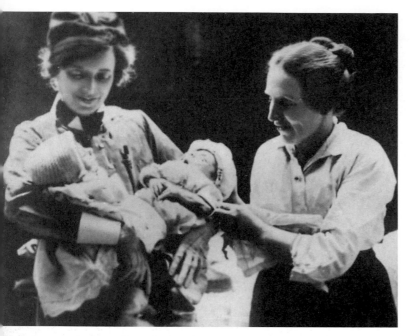

This postcard of a Queen's nurse and new baby is another from the sets produced in memory of the late patron, Queen Alexandra, and sold to raise funds for the Institute. Picture c.1900s.

that public bodies were calling upon them to do special preventative work. In Brighton, for example, the DNA assigned all their nurses to dressing and ambulance stations in view of the possibility of bombardment. St Helen's, Lancashire had their nurses helping inoculate soldiers against typhoid, whilst across the country district nurses helped care for wounded and convalescent soldiers. In the London district of Paddington and Marylebone, the nurses had an enormous area to cover, including a resident in Willesden, as well as Poor Law cases. Nurses were allotted to various minor injury centres in the two boroughs, besides undertaking work at the Marylebone tuberculosis dispensary. In Cheltenham, one of the QNs voluntarily attended the local Mothers' Club on two afternoons a week, and once a month she visited those children who were over one year old but under school age, if necessary going to see them at home.

District nurses working on the home front often found themselves in dangerous situations, and nowhere was this better exemplified than by Nurse E.M. Vicary and her fellow QNs in the nurses home in Scarborough at eight in the morning on 16 December 1914, when the town came under bombardment from a German ship:

> 'Quite suddenly the sound of a gun was heard. It was most alarming as the whole house vibrated and it seemed as if every window must come in …. The shells came quite quickly and the noise was deafening … directly the shelling stopped the second time, two of us went out to see if we could render any assistance … The St John ambulance men were astir and we saw some stretcher cases being taken to the hospital … We went round to see as many of our patients as we could, some of the poor old folk were in a terrible way, but not any of our people were injured …'

By October 1914, a large proportion of QNs were working in the territorial hospitals, amongst them Superintendents and Assistant Superintendents whose skills had to be subsumed to doing almost probationers work in the wards. This was brought to the attention of the QVJIN Council by the Executive Committee in May 1915, who remarked that these professional women 'were urgently needed in organizing the new schemes for maternity and child welfare

National shell-filling factory, possibly Leeds, c.1915.

which had been brought forward by the Local Government Board and the Board of Education'. But the *QNM* was certain that:

> 'One and all are cheerfully accepting the situation, remembering that they too are soldiers of the King and must submit to discipline…'

Work for the district nurses on the remote Scottish Highlands and Islands carried on much as before the war. The Highlands and Islands medical service continued to flourish, and between 1913 and 1916 the number of parish or DNAs increased fivefold. Constitutions were written to specifically include the treatment of patients under the scheme in order to become eligible for grants.

It was 1917 before the inhabitants of Burra Isle had a district nurse, and in her first year she dealt successfully with 'epidemics of chicken pox and influenza, many cases of blood poisoning from fish-hooks, as well as fourteen maternity cases', whilst the nurse on Lewis, recounted the amusing tale of struggling with a hen and a confinement:

> 'After I had prepared all my things the hen flew down right in the middle and sent them flying into the mud and the fire. I then told my patient she must get into bed, which she did, telling me that I must not disturb the hen as she had her nest in the bed. I now do my puerperium in the morning with the hen at her back on the nest.'

District nurses at home had the additional burden of undertaking public health work: By 1916 Gloucestershire county nursing association reported that, 'of the seventy-two DNAs affiliated to the county nursing association, sixty-four are co-operating in this scheme for Public Health Work'. A year later, there were also sixteen infant welfare centres in the county attended by the district nurses, where mothers could have their babies weighed and ask for advice on health and feeding.

By December 1915, there were 557 QNs on the QAIMNS reserve list, and an unknown number with the TFNS, but even these experienced district nurses, who were well were used to adapting and improvising in difficult conditions, found the conditions abroad challenging.

These pictures appeared in the *QNM* in 1915, and highlight the danger of nursing in Scarborough.

One nurse wrote in October 1915 of how 'every drop of water has to be boiled, even to drink, and this place teems with typhoid and nearly every other disease under the sun'. Miss Elizabeth Curtis, who for many years was Superintendent of the Hammersmith QNs, became Matron of the Urgency Cases Hospital at Bar-le-Duc, France, the only British unit in the Meuse. The mobile surgical ambulance opened its doors to badly wounded French soldiers on 23 March 1915, and during the six months the hospital was located there, it admitted 838 patients, performed 364 operations and suffered thirty-six deaths. Being far from the front line, the field hospital came to specialise in the treatment of fractures, until it was moved to a new location, close to the fighting line, at the Chateau Faux Miroir at Revigny, in August 1915. It took two weeks to build barrack accommodation in a bare field for the wounded, and Miss Curtis and her staff had to contend with all sorts of difficulties, as she recorded:

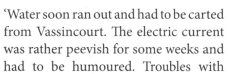

Flora Jackson, a Queen's district nurse, was destined for St Kilda, but the island was evacuated before her arrival. *c.1915. Courtesy of the Royal College of Nursing.*

'Water soon ran out and had to be carted from Vassincourt. The electric current was rather peevish for some weeks and had to be humoured. Troubles with washing, heating and catering presented themselves in turn, and were duly overcome … The ambulance train from the Argonne was stopped each day at Revigny for us and we were allowed to select our own cases.'

Miss Curtis resigned her position in December 1915, returning home, via Paris, to inspect some of the ambulances, and then taking up a post as an examiner with a Dr Hinds Howell.

There was plenty of scope for district nurses to undertake maternity work abroad as well, with one nurse writing from a barely-ready maternity hospital in France in late 1914:

'We had patients rushed in … and babies are born if not on the floor it is owing to what shall I say – good management? … We had a big operation on Monday, and "twins" on Wednesday, one of them died and the other is my special care, in fact I seem to run around with him tucked under my arm.'

Another, Miss Ubsdell, a QN who had worked at Sandridge and Riverhead, Kent, before taking up war service, was with the Friends' Expedition at Chalons-sur-Marne, France, when she rescued a mother, her newly delivered baby and her three other children from a hole in the ground – all that remained of a bombarded house, which was reached by a rope ladder:

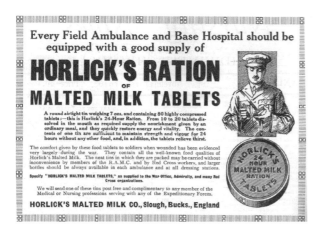

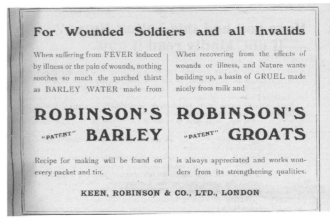

Advertisers took advantage of the needs of servicemen with advertisements in the nursing press.
Nursing Notes, November 1916.

> 'Both the poor mother and her children were covered with vermin, and the only garment the mother had on was a chemise. All the food these unfortunate creatures had was a little bread.'

Many nurses showed extreme courage and went far beyond the call of duty to reach those who needed their care. Violetta Thurstan had been Queen's County Superintendent for Yorkshire West Riding for three years before she joined the British Red Cross in 1913. Called up in August 1914, her first post was in Brussels, in a hospital improvised from a fire-station, with 130 beds in six large wards, before she and two other sisters volunteered to go to Charleroi, and then on to a Red Cross hospital in the country beyond Beaumont, where she was subsequently appointed Matron:

> 'The confusion that reigned was indescribable … it is a dreadful nightmare to look back at. Bloodstained uniforms hastily cut off the soldiers were lying on the floor – half-open packets of dressings were on every locker; basins of dirty water or disinfectant had not been emptied; men were moaning with pain, calling for water, begging that their dressings might be done again…And the cannon never ceased booming. Among the other miseries of that night was the dreadful shortage of all hospital supplies, and the scarcity of food for the men.'

When the Germans ordered all the English doctors and nurses to leave, Violetta and her nurses were taken under armed escort by train to the Danish border, and once they were safe in Copenhagen, had their offer to volunteer for the Russian Red Cross accepted. They arrived in Russia in October 1915 and worked with a community of Russian sisters in Smolney, where they underwent 'instructions in Russian and their methods of First Aid' which were very different to home. What troubled her most was:

> '… their custom of giving strong narcotic or stimulating drugs indiscriminately, such

as morphine, codeine, camphor, or ether without doctors' orders. When untrained Sisters and inexperienced dressers do this (which constantly happens) the results are sometimes deplorable.'

From there she travelled to Warsaw before joining Prince Volkonsky's Flying Ambulance Surgery Service at the height of the battle for Lodz.

There were a number of district nurses who found themselves on the Eastern front, including one who recalled in 1917 how she had done 'real active service'. Having arrived in Alexandria in 1915, she had responded to a request for volunteers for Lemnos, Greece, where conditions were 'very unfavourable'. Back in Egypt some months later, they pitched their camp:

'in the desert within a short distance of the enemy, about fifteen miles…. The heat was terrific all through, and we worked on the field in a temperature of 130° and 140° many days.'

There was also danger at sea, as QN Miss Mary Stevenson discovered in March 1917, when she was nursing on His Majesty's Hospital Ship, *Asturias*. The staff had just finished discharging 1000 wounded men at Southampton, and was en route to Avonmouth when she was torpedoed by a German U-boat. Miss Stevenson escaped onto on a little boat but it capsized as it was lowered into the water, and she was flung out and drifted away.

Another QN, Miss Meirion Evans, was in the Mediterranean when the ship she was on was torpedoed and, unlike the *Asturias*, sank within an hour. Sixty-six nursing staff were lowered onto life boats and spent three hours in rough seas with waves coming over their heads. She was grateful that 'they were picked up by an ally's destroyer … we were at last landed and stayed in convents: the people were very good to us'.

January 1918 found Miss Gertrude Line writing from Salonika, reporting on her experiences, which included her all-night journey on a 'dirty train infested with mosquitoes' to reach the 37th General Hospital' where the patients poured in day and night, and where they soon had 1,500 patients. Despite the sick suffering from the worst forms of malaria, 'the death toll was very low indeed'. Once the unit was divided up she found herself 'by the sea and still nursing Serbs,' but by then 'Salonika had little or no attractions', and the nurses were 'even denied the shopping expeditions they had promised themselves'. To compensate for this, she was delighted to have met a lot of QNs she knew from Cardiff, some of whom were doing refugee and midwifery work.

Tented accommodation overseas. The nurses' quarters were in the round tents, with access across duckboards, enabling them to get around in the often very wet and muddy conditions.

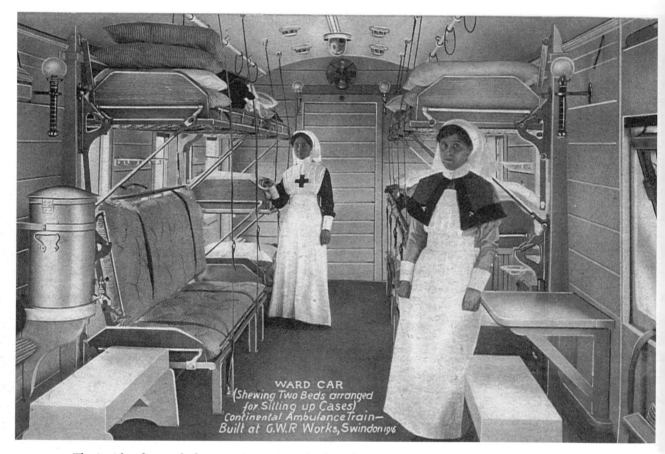

WARD CAR
(Shewing Two Beds arranged
for Sitting up Cases)
Continental Ambulance Train-
Built at G.W.R Works, Swindon 1916

The inside of an ambulance train carriage, built at the Great Western railway works, Swindon. Several QNs who were reservists with the QAINMS served on these trains, which transported wounded men from the military hospitals to the ports for transfer home.

All in all, the work was mentally and physically exhausting, with very little respite, but one Scottish QN wrote of how, following a retreat and evacuation in France, some fifty medical staff had been put on an ambulance train on 30 March 1918 and were 'taken to a lovely quiet place where they enjoyed a week's rest'. A spell as a nurse in charge of a Casualty Clearing Station followed but despite the excitement she 'longed more than ever for the War to finish'.

Not surprisingly, many district nurses received official recognition for their wartime contribution, although Miss Tait McKay wrote that there was no greater reward than 'the gratitude of the tens of thousands of patients who have passed through [their] hands'. She herself was awarded the Royal Red Cross (First Class) in January 1916 and received the decoration from the King at Buckingham Palace the following month.

Nurse Barnes, a Staff Nurse with the TFNS, received a 'mention' in the *Edinburgh Gazette* on 5 June 1916 and was awarded the Royal Red Cross, (Second Class), as was Florence Nightingale Shore, one of Florence Nightingale's goddaughters, whilst Miss Florence Filkin, QAIMNS(R), formerly

QN Mary Stevenson, was aboard His Majesty's Hospital Ship, *Asturias* on 20 March 1917, en route from Avonmouth to Southampton, having just unloaded a cargo of 1,000 wounded men, when it was torpedoed by a German U-boat. Thirty-one people were killed, but she was rescued from a small boat, and spent a week in a military hospital recovering. She recalled later that it was a mercy that she lost consciousness, for it was dark, icy cold, and terrifying, and she had no idea how long she drifted for. *QNM,* 1917, p.35.

Superintendent of the Cheshire County Nursing Association, was mentioned in despatches for 'gallant and distinguished service in the field'. Miss Gertrude Line, wrote of being:

'the proud wearer of a Serbian Medal (the Order of Samaritan). The Diploma is as nice as the Medal, and when translated reads: "In the name of Peter 1st., by the Grace of God and will of the people King of Serbia, Alexander Prince Regent, I, Minister of war, decorate Nursing Sister G.L.Line with the Cross of our Samaritan for attention to our sick and wounded in the wars of 1914-1917"'.

Yet another example was the award, in late 1916, of the Silver Medaille d'Honneur des Epidemiés

The Royal Red Cross was instituted as a decoration by Queen Victoria by royal warrant of 23 April 1883 for award to ladies who showed special devotion while nursing the sick and wounded of the Army and Navy. In November 1915, the Royal Red Cross was expanded to two classes: First Class, or Member (RRC); and Second Class, or Associate (ARRC). The obverse of this Royal Red Cross, Second Class, which is made of silver, bears the date 1883.

by the French government to Miss Turnell, Inspector of the Scottish Branch, for her work under the French Flag Nursing Corps since the outbreak of the conflict in 1914.

The first name to be inscribed on the Roll of Honour of the QVJIN was that of Miss Louisa Jordan, a QN from Buckhaven, Fife who served as a Staff Sister with the Scottish Women's Hospital unit at Kraguievatz, Serbia from 1 December 1914. Tragically, she caught typhus from one of the lady doctors she was treating, and died from the disease in March 1915.

The interior of a hospital barge showing the cargo hold converted into a functioning ward. The barges transported wounded soldiers along the French waterways enabling them to be transferred direct to hospital ships. A number of QNs were amongst the QAINMS reservists who nursed on the barges.

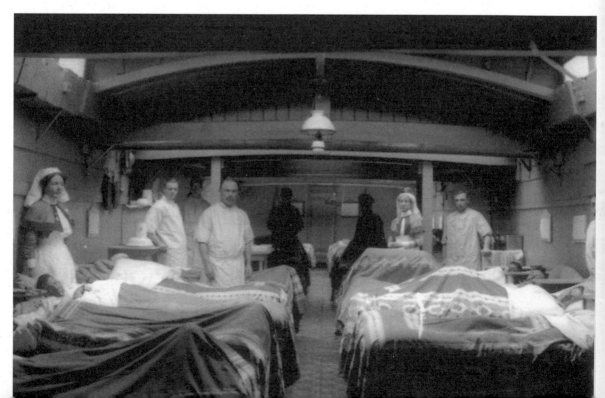

Chapter 5

DISTRICT NURSING BETWEEN THE WARS

DESPITE THE RELIEF that years of conflict were at an end, war weariness and a devastating influenza epidemic in 1918 exerted huge pressure on the district nursing service at home, Gloucestershire County Nursing Association reported that many of the county's district nurses 'worked incessantly, day and night,' and two of them, 'Nurse S. Wright, who was at Mickleton for some years, and was loved and respected by all, and Nurse Enos, after only three months on her district - she was young, bright, and devoted to her work,' succumbed to the disease. The QNs covering Brighton, Hove and Preston treated 376 cases of influenza during 1918, and often visited patients two, three or even four times a day. In Leicester, the district nurses struggled along for the first two weeks of October 1918 without any extra help, working for between nine and eleven hours a day. Just as they thought they could not carry on, help arrived. The

A postcard showing the funeral procession of a victim of the Spanish Flu epidemic in Dover, 1918.

local medical officer of health sent all the health visitors, and when the schools closed, all the school nurses joined them. Besides the eight extra nurses, a local newspaper appeal brought forth a band of voluntary helpers, who variously made jellies, custards and puddings for the convalescents, cleaned or sat with patients at night time. It was a great relief when a ward was opened at the fever hospital for bad cases and for those who it was impossible to nurse at home, for some of the nurses had succumbed to a light dose of flu, and their numbers were reduced to two. The February 1919 epidemic, was, according to the Leicester nurse, not so severe, nor was it so depressing to nurse, as they had more recoveries.

If the flu epidemic was not enough, the organisation was already suffering from depleted numbers. By then, most DNAs were asking for a subscription of one penny a week, 4s 4d per annum, with a midwifery fee of 15s. District nurses in the remote parts of the Scottish Highlands and Islands were paid more than the average wage to compensate for the conditions they faced, but the QNs in particular were not, according the Dewar Report, always the most adaptable. In isolated areas, for example, it was not unusual for the nurse to have to stay with a maternity case for several days if there were no relatives to help. Whilst the established, but less well qualified cottage and maternity nurses were happy to do so, some of the QNs were reluctant to follow suit.

District nurses on the steps of the Edinburgh District Nurses Home of Queen Victoria's Jubilee Institute for Nurses. The District Nurses Home was based at the headquarters of the QVJIN at Castle Terrace, Edinburgh. c.1930. *Courtesy of the Royal College of Nursing Archive.*

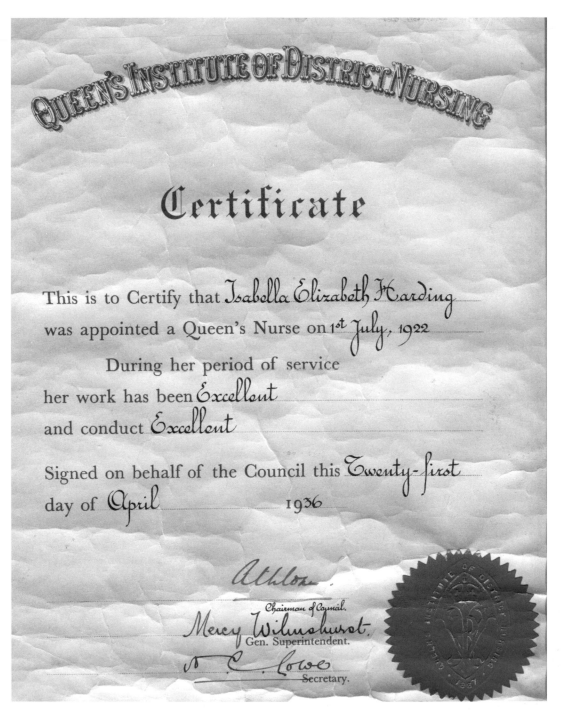

Isabella Harding's certificate of appointment, 1922.

By 1928, the courses provided by the Institute reflected the wide range of work and were very comprehensive, including both theoretical and practical elements. For the former, there were lectures on hygiene, school medical service, sanitary law, elementary physiology, notifiable diseases, maternity, legal enactments, venereal disease, infant and child welfare, tuberculosis, diseases of the eye, ear and throat, social problems and elementary economics. The practical element included visiting and clinical work in tuberculosis and eye cases. Mary Quain, the Lady Dudley nurse in Carraroe from 1937 to 1943, had to visit tubercular and other ill patients in their homes, to change dressings and make them comfortable, to carry out health inspections in the local schools and advise on child welfare. In theory, she was supposed to have one half-day free each week but, in practice, she was always available and had no time off, even on Sundays. Frequently a week passed without her getting to bed, catching naps in patients' homes waiting for labour to progress.

What might have appeared an issue in 1919 was certainly not a problem in West Sussex in 1934, for here the district nurses undertook all the necessary public health duties in addition to

A district nurse helps a doctor perform a tracheotomy on a child with diphtheria in a house in the 1950s.

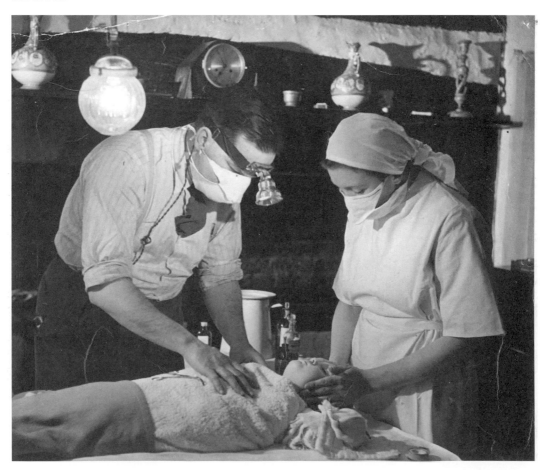

their general and midwifery work. The county nursing association was served by seventy-three DNAs and other than the coastal fringe, was a largely agricultural county with many isolated farmhouses and cottages. Every house in the county was within a circle served by some district nurse, and the benefits of the service to mothers in particular were described in an article in *Town and Country News* in Spring 1934:

> 'The mother is not worried and her time wasted by a number of different visitors, and the nurse is able to follow the fortunes of each child from the pre-natal stage to the end of its school days. From the time the mother 'books' the nurse to make arrangements for her confinement, ante-natal care ensures, as far as possible, a safe passage into this world for the infant a clear start in life. On the fourteenth day after the birth the nurse returns to her role as health visitor, and weighs and examines the child at regular intervals up to the school age…As school nurse she sees the child at regular intervals for medical, dental and general cleanliness inspections.'

Dental morning at the school and minor ailment clinic, Chichester, where the district nurse worked part time. *QNM,* March 1934, p.70.

Delivering babies was a regular part of the district nurses role, and in 1924, QVJI nurses attended ten per cent of home births in England and Wales, and by 1925 district nursing was available to seventy-five per cent of the population. When the first annual report of the QVJI Irish branch was published in 1925, it showed how the 195 QNs and others in affiliated districts across the country had each made an average number of 4,196 visits during the previous year. In total, they had dealt with 27,396 medical and surgical cases, 1,064 midwifery cases and 51,106 maternity and child welfare cases. The cost of district and midwifery training was put at £35 per nurse, and following the district training, QNs had to sign an agreement to work for one year at either St Patrick's or St Lawrence's in Dublin, before choosing their preferred location.

Reports in the nursing press about the opening of new maternity homes included one in March, Cambridgeshire on 28 April 1924, which served as a home for the three district nurses with two maternity wards attached. At a cost of about £4,000 the nurses must have been thrilled to have individual 'furnished bed-sitting rooms, somewhat in the Newnham College style … hot and cold water … and central heating'. Visitors at the open day commended the 'artistic furnishing and labour-saving arrangements'. The district nurses in Cardiff were thrilled when, in 1924, the past treasurer, Mr Mullins, presented the nurses home with a three-valve wireless set for use in their sitting room, enabling them to listen to 'the varied programmes provide by the British Broadcasting Corporation'. The superintendent was provided with a headphone for her personal use. Even more important perhaps was the installation of electricity in the home.

Getting around their districts still proved challenging for many district nurses, as twenty-year

This postcard, showing 'a happy group of QNs with twins' was published in 1926, and is from the collection produced in memory of Queen Alexandra.

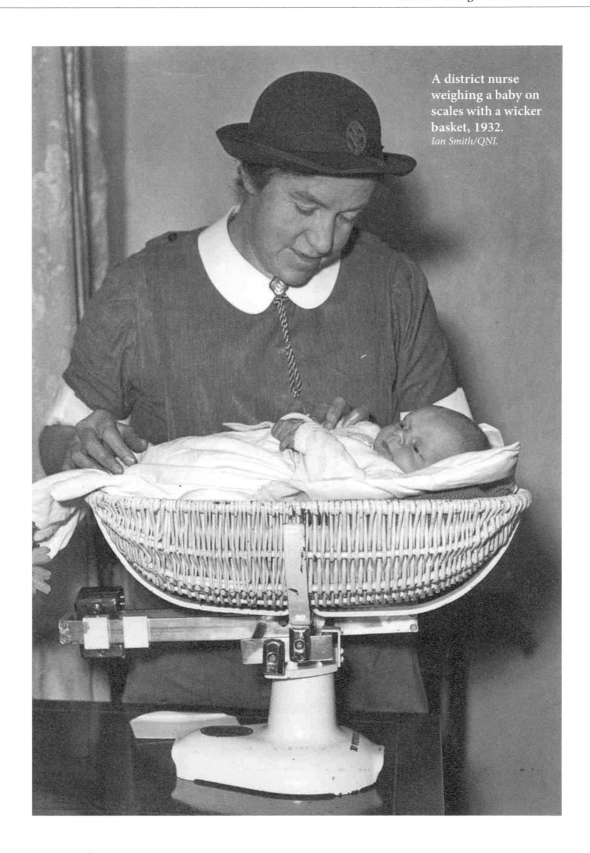

A district nurse weighing a baby on scales with a wicker basket, 1932.
Ian Smith/QNI.

old Nurse Hannah Mills Evans discovered when she joined Montgomeryshire Nursing Association in September 1919. She served the community of Llanfair Caereinion and the surrounding upland area of rural Wales until 1964, and before she eventually had a car, regularly covered 1,200 miles each month, travelling along country roads and rough farm tracks to visit her patients. Like her counterparts, she walked, rode on horseback or used a bicycle to get around.

Advances in transport helped Nurse Evans, when she was provided with a motor cycle in 1923, by which time the *QNM* was advising district nurses on the different types of auxiliary cycle engines that were available.

This district nurse's home was named in memory QN Florence Nightingale Shore, one of Florence Nightingale's god-daughters. She had a distinguished career, not least as a nurse working with the French Red Cross and QAIMNS(R) in casualty clearing stations, hospitals and on ambulance trains in France during the First World War, for which she was awarded the RRC (Second Class). She was fatally wounded on a train journey from Hastings on 12 June 1920, and died four days later.

Those who were not experienced motor cyclists were advised against the French Cyclotracteur, with its 1¾ horse power front engine, for it was, in their opinion, 'an awkward contrivance to manage when going round corners'. For novices, they recommended:

'a machine with an auxiliary engine mounted on the rear wheel. The nurse's bag, lighter than the engine and the petrol container, must go on the handle bar, tiresome as this may seem. And it should be so fixed that it will not swing over to one side going round corners at the smart pace at which an auxiliary travels.'

A car was eventually purchased in 1935, with £10 a year provided for its upkeep. Brighton did not buy an Autocycle until 1938, paying £40 16s for the vehicle, and it was not long before the secretary of Poole DNA was highlighting some of the practical

QN Flora Ferguson, who originated from Glendale, was the first motorised district nurse in Inverness-shire. Stratherrick DNA bought this motorcycle in August 1926 with a grant from the Highlands and Islands Medical Service.
Courtesy of the Highland Archive Service, (Ref: GB232/ D582/B/1/23).

Elizabeth McPhee was another motorized QN and her district covered the parishes of Kintail and Glensheil, Scotland. 1926. Eilean Donan Castle, Skye, can be seen in the background.

An unidentified district nurse with her rather battered bicycle, c. 1930s.

disadvantages of the machine. Oil and petrol were prone to seep out of the tank and soak clothes, feet and legs were exposed to wind and rain, and despite the flap on the front mud guard, mud and rain were thrown back off the front wheel. Her solution was to design a combined leg-guard and engine shield made of lightweight sheet iron, which any competent sheet metal worker could make using her drawings and instructions.

In 1933, nearly fifty years after it was founded, the Portsmouth Victoria Association for Nursing the Sick Poor was very busy meeting the needs of a growing city. The city boundary had been extended, which resulted in an increase in demand, which could only be met by employing an additional nurse. An extra car was purchased, for without it the district could not be covered efficiently. The number of cases attended kept increasing, from 2,018 in 1931

This district nurse had to call upon the services of the local farmer and his tractor to help her reach her patient.

This rural district nurse had a car, which made visiting a patient much easier. circa 1950s.
Courtesy of Barnet Saidman/QNI.

to 2,095 in 1932, whilst the number of visits went up from 50,084 to 54,948. The daily routine in Portsmouth was replicated in district nurses' homes across the country; a meeting with the matron to get ready for their morning round, starting at 8.45 am. The matron, Miss Johnson, would have a sheaf of slips of papers with particulars of new cases which she distributed amongst her nurses according to the district. Portsmouth was divided into thirteen districts, each nurse had a heavy workload, which meant that some could only be visited on alternate days, rather than on a daily basis. The Eastney nurse had seventeen cases as well at the barracks, an unrealistic morning's work, and was fortunate to have several of her patients taken over by one of the less busy nurses. Rounds were made using a bicycle, regardless of the weather. The nurse was due back at the Home for lunch at 1.30 pm but was often delayed. In between going out on the evening round, which started at 4.45 pm, the nurse had to report on every case to the matron, keep her case books up to date, attend lectures, replenish her bag, and if she was really lucky, have time for a rest. This was the time to call on new cases, undertake weekly

Bicycles and a car are the mode of transport for these inner-city district nurses as they leave the nurses home to go out on their rounds. c.1950s.

blanket baths and revisit acutely ill patients.

By the mid-1920s, uniform changes were in the air once again. A coat-frock style dress was designed with a loose belt, the Holland apron had no gathers, and there was an option to replace that with an apron if desired. The coat was cut 'so as to give more width across the chest … the straw or felt hat is of an approved design, trimmed with a navy ribbon with a bow at the side'. Black shoes and stockings were de rigeur. Worrying about what cap to wear for cycling, a topic of discussion in early magazines, was far less important than how to keep dry, but nurses were offered sound advice on a suitable mackintosh in February 1921:

> 'One made of vulcanised rubber will be very satisfactory. It will not crack, but leatherette gaiters should be worn to prevent rain trickling into the boots. One can be procured from Currie Thomson & Co, Jamaica Street, Glasgow. The cost, two months ago, was £2 10s'.

District nurses meeting with their superintendent, 1930s.

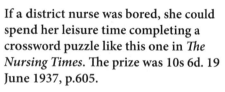

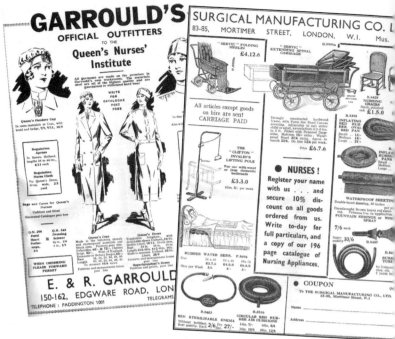

If a district nurse was bored, she could spend her leisure time completing a crossword puzzle like this one in *The Nursing Times*. The prize was 10s 6d. 19 June 1937, p.605.

A uniform advert from June 1936. Advertisements like these for surgical and nursing equipment appeared regularly in the district nursing magazines. *QNM, September 1936.*

By 1926, another QN was extolling the virtues of a garment made of:

> 'guaranteed fine quality wool cashmere … it is provided with "Three way" collar which can be either turned down or buttoned up to the neck, or the collar may be turned up with a flap buttoning across the throat … The price is £2 15s … and can be obtained from Messrs Boyd Cooper, 4 George Street Hanover Square London'.

The ever-essential fund raising continued and ranged from the grand to the humble. At the top end of the scale was a Charity Ball, held at Lansdowne House, London on 26 April 1923, by kind permission of Mr Gordon Selfridge, and hosted by Marchioness Curzon. The patrons included the Duchesses of Sutherland, Somerset, Norfolk and Grafton as well as Prince Henry, Prince George and King Alfonso of Spain. Guests paid three guineas a head, drank champagne all night and danced to the music provided by Paul Whiteman and his orchestra. At a more modest level, the children of Llantrisant, Wales, gave a concert in April 1921 to raise funds for their recently established DNA, and as the *QNM* reported 'their efforts were very successful, and they realised £40, a very nice sum to hand over in these difficult times', whilst Portsmouth were not alone in holding annual flag days. But small collections were never enough, and it was once again a royal patron that brought financial salvation. In 1926, following the death of their much-loved patron, Queen Alexandra, the now-renamed Queen's Institute of District Nursing (QIDN, 1925), inaugurated a national memorial fund with the approval of King George V and Queen Mary, who became the next patron. All over Britain mayors, provosts and other local dignitaries exerted themselves to boost the fund, and by 1928, the grand sum of £ 233,086 12s 6d had been raised for the QIDN.

In addition to this, Mrs Elsie Wagg, a member of the Council, invented the fund-raising National Garden Scheme, founded by the Institute in 1927. She had the novel idea of asking the public to open their private gardens to the

A postcard showing QNs at work. This postcard was published in 1926, and is another from the sets produced in memory of the late Queen, and sold to raise funds for the Institute

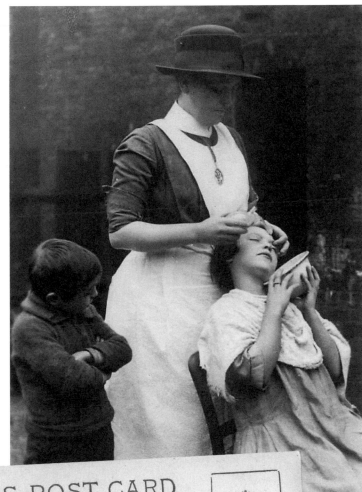

TUCK'S POST CARD
CARTE POSTALE

By Appointment   THE NATIONAL MEMORIAL TO QUEEN ALEXANDRA.

Please keep the Ball rolling and help the Fund. Buy a Packet of these Cards (6 for 1/-) and send to friends. To be obtained from Local Nursing Associations or Queen Victoria's Jubilee Institute for Nurses, 58, Victoria St., S.W.1.

Copyright London   Printed in England   Raphael Tuck & Sons' "REAL PHOTOGRAPH" POSTCARD.   ART PUBLISHERS TO THEIR MAJESTIES THE KING & QUEEN.

A rural district nurses home, Nightingale Cottage, Chipstead, Surrey, 1930s.

public, and to make a small charge for entry. In June 1927, 349 gardens opened, including Sandringham in Norfolk and Blenheim Palace in Oxfordshire, with members of the public paying one shilling each to enter. The scheme was so successful it was continued into September by which time over six hundred gardens had opened and over £8,000 had been raised.

In the years that followed, a network of county organisers was established in order to encourage garden owners to open their gardens on an annual basis. As well as the royal family, the Royal Horticultural Society, *Country Life* magazine, the British Broadcasting Corporation and the Automobile Association were all early supporters. By 1930, the number of open gardens reached 900 and Sir Winston Churchill and Vita Sackville-West were amongst those who opened their private gardens to the public. And as a way of raising awareness of their work, in the early 1920s the QVJIN arranged, with the co-operation of Mr Selfridge, to have a display in the window of his grand Oxford Street store.

Raising money to fund the organisation and services was a perpetual problem, and by the 1930s, most DNAs had turned to the support of provident schemes. The QIDN, as it was renamed in 1928, produced a short film encouraging people to subscribe to their local association, enabling them to receive district nursing care at a reduced price. Shirley Morris, the secretary of the Leicester DNA was especially successful, when she advised charging one penny a fortnight to subscribers, while those who were not subscribers would be charged 1s 6d for each visit by a nurse. The arithmetic was obviously compelling and 60,000 workers in Leicester were subscribers in 1929. Over 80,000 home visits were made by nurses in the city that year, income rose from £3,000 to £9,000 per year and the number of nurses employed rose from 18 to 30.

The gardens at Balls Park, Hertford, with their eighteenth century formal gardens and park covering 25 hectares, were amongst the earliest to open to the public as part of the National Garden Scheme.

Many city nurses lived away from their districts and were able to maintain an independent private life, but this was a luxury not afforded to the rural or island district nurse. They were also fortunate in that they generally had easy access to a doctor, and even to a hospital, and although the nurse was not accountable to the medical practitioner, her caseload was often determined by the referrals that he made, rather than by direct calls from patients.

Then there was the question of the relationship between them, which could sometimes be difficult, especially if the doctor felt the nurse was taking over his work. The QIDN rules were

Tottenham QNs' Home as it was when it was newly built in 1938, with white rendered walls and green ceramic roof tiles. During the 1930s DNAs began to build modern bespoke nurses' homes, designed for comfort, space and clinical needs, a trend that was taken up again after the Second World War.

Hackney Queen's Nursing Association, London, celebrating the 50th anniversary of the QNI in 1937.

clear, and prohibited a QN from dispensing medicines that were only to be prescribed by a medical man, so when district nurse Miss Hunt refused to stop doing so, Dr Huxley, the chairman of Bagley Wood DNA, had no choice but to have her dismissed.

Whilst the rapport between the two professions may, at times, have been difficult, the district nurse remained a firm favourite with her child patients, evidenced by a poignant competition entry written by a child in Leeds in June 1939. In the essay, a child from Holbeck wrote:

'District nurses go to your house because they want you to get better. One day a district nurse came to me when I had rheumatism and measles ... I like the district nurse very much indeed. She would tell me

The district nurses' home in Brenchley, Kent, 1930s.

Queen Elizabeth, then the Duchess of York, visiting Castle Terrace, Edinburgh, in 1929.

This postcard of Queen Mary was produced after she became patron of the QIDN in 1925, following the death of Queen Alexandra. This postcard was published in 1926, and is another from the sets produced in memory of the late Queen, and sold to raise funds for the Institute.

stories when my brothers were at school and my mother at the workshop.'

He also wrote that 'They are kind to you and they are healthy and strong', attributes that were to stand them, and the people they cared for, in good stead during the years of war that were to follow.

These QNs were being presented to the royal entourage at Holyrood House, Edinburgh in 1934.

Here, Queen Mary is seen presenting Long Service awards at the Jubilee Review on 16 June 1937, commemorating the fiftieth anniversary of the organisation.

QNs at Buckingham Palace on 16 June 1937, for the fiftieth anniversary Jubilee Review.

Chapter 6

THE SECOND WORLD WAR, 1939-1945

'The Council of the QIDN expressed its deep appreciation of the magnificent way in which QNs and county nurses have worked untiringly, and often at great danger to themselves, to lessen the distress of those who, in Great Britain and Ireland, have suffered enemy action…. the nurses everywhere have shown themselves to be as heroic and selfless as any of those who are helping to defend the country, and the Council is very proud of them.' *(QNM, March 1941)*

AT THE OUTSET of the Second World War there were 4,566 QNs working in Great Britain and Ireland, and even though they were actively discouraged from volunteering for active service, in sharp contrast to the previous conflict, there was still a sharp decline in their numbers. As part of the home defence system, district nursing was a front-line occupation, but the demands varied geographically, and at different times during the war. Many districts were seemingly untouched, and whilst they escaped the fall out of bombing campaigns, they still had to deal with stress-related illnesses and a heavier workload due to staff shortages, the loss of medical colleagues and the relocation of patients from endangered urban areas.

The new roles that district nurses undertook varied widely. Evacuation left some without a post, as most schools and welfare centres were closed, besides which financial pressure meant that many DNAs could no longer afford

Magazine cover, 1946. Even though the war was over, the shortage of paper continued, the magazine became thinner and there were hardly any advertisements included.

The relics of bomb damage in Birmingham were still evident in the late 1960s. *Courtesy of Frances Tebbutt.*

to employ a nurse. Others sought work elsewhere, some resigned, whilst many were loaned to local authorities to help run air-raid shelters and first-aid posts. There were also those who joined the Armed and Civilian Defence Services. Not surprisingly, this exacerbated the shortage of district nurses, especially in London, which was only halted by the introduction of the 1943 Control of Engagement Order, which effectively prevented nurses leaving their posts.

Unlike the First World War, accounts in the nursing press from district nurses who did join the forces were few and far between but included one, in June 1940, from a QN who had arrived in France with QAIMNS on 11 November 1939. She described how, in her hospital, 'our lads are poorly housed for the most part and being unused to roughing it on stone floors and badly ventilated rooms, fell victims to many ailments', including rubella. The hospital had no hot-water system, so that:

> 'when boiling water was needed for a dozen or so inhalations, four hourly, fifty-six gargles T.D.S. (three times a day) antiphlogistine to be heated, two-hourly feeds to be made, patients to be blanket bathed, everything had to be managed on one very poor gas ring and a very "tricky" Primus stove. You will believe me when I say we were kept "at it" …When hostilities began in real earnest, and people from all over the place were coming through our port after the evacuation of Dunkirk, we had to become a casualty clearing station instead of a base hospital, and send cases fit to travel straight back to

Evacuee children arriving at Newbold Farm, Monmouthshire, in the 1940s. For city children, a rural environment like this was a total shock, and many were very unhappy indeed.

England. Several hundred sisters came to our hospital for the night on their way home. Many had lost all their kit. Some whom I knew personally had lost their hospital ship; it went down at Dunkirk. They were thankful for a mattress on the floor to sleep on after many days and nights of harassing experiences. Once a week for half an hour we were ordered to work in our gas masks. This was a good idea, but not a welcome one, but it was a humorous sight to see us wearing our veil caps on the top of them … For over a fortnight before we actually evacuated we were told to be ready to leave at a moment's notice. We were being raided every night. Sometimes two or three times a night we were down in the cellar in the pitch dark with our hand luggage ready for a quick "get away" if necessary.'

The P & O SS *Strathallan*, having been painted over in grey and requisitioned by the Ministry of Shipping, for service as a troop transport ship on 4 February 1940. *Courtesy of the State Library of Victoria.*

The gallantry of Miss Olive Stewardson, formally a QN in Scarborough and Doncaster, serving with the QAIMNS in 1943, warranted an article in the *QNM* for she was amongst the sisters who refused to leave their transport ship, the SS *Strathallan*, after it was attacked and set on fire by a torpedo on 21 December 1942. But it was a lengthy feature in the *Daily Express* on 13 January 1943, written by James Wellard, one of their reporters who was travelling on the ship, which captured her real heroism:

> 'As I write this we are sinking. Fire has broken out below decks. The crump of a torpedo smacking the side of a big ship when you are fast asleep in your berth is a sound you don't want to hear more than once in your life. We, the nurses and soldiers, American and British, heard it in the night. When 29 year old Olive Stewardson from Yorkshire and 26 year old Julie Kerr, who is Irish, heard it they knew they had a duty to perform. They are Queen Alexandra nurses. That duty was in the troops' hospital deep down in the bowels of the ship. The rest of us stumbled up the dark stairs to our boat stations. We stood, some of us frightened, some of us singing, all of us calm and disciplined as befits soldiers. Sisters Stewardson and Kerr went down below decks while we went up. In the ship's hospital were five stretcher cases. The two sisters got them ready and saw them carried to safety. By this time the crowded lifeboats were away from the ship. There was no chance now for the nurses to leave except on rafts. Floating on a raft in a sea covered

with fuel oil is the last resort, but the nurses had no thought of leaving. There was more work to do. Casualties were coming into that little hospital below decks. Sailors and soldiers covered in fuel oil and exhausted were being brought in every minute. Sisters Stewardson and Kerr carried on. They cut off the men's clothing, massaged them, hot water bottles at their feet. Late the next day the sisters came on deck, their work done. They found the sun shining bright and warm. The ship was listing 20 degrees. …. Here is the story Sisters Stewardson and Kerr told me – "When the torpedo hit we got dressed, put on our tin hats, collected our greatcoats and went to the troops' hospital on the lower deck. We found the medical officer and orderlies already there, strapping patients to the stretchers. Two of the men had broken legs. As soon as we had taken care of the stretcher cases we went upstairs. Then the casualties from the lifeboats and rafts were brought in. We were asked to go down to the hospital and take care of them. They were the soldiers and sailors who had jumped to the rafts; they were covered in fuel oil. Most of them were exhausted from exposure. We took off their clothes and rubbed them, and did what we could. It was late next day - five hours later, when we came up on the top deck. They wrapped us in warm blankets. And here we are.'"

The two nursing sisters were amongst nearly 300 nurses on board at the outset of the journey. All those remaining on board were lifted to safety before the *Strathallan* sank.

The need to be adaptable was ingrained in women when they undertook their district

This district nurse was also a health visitor, and is seen here visiting a Herefordshire hop garden in the 1940s.

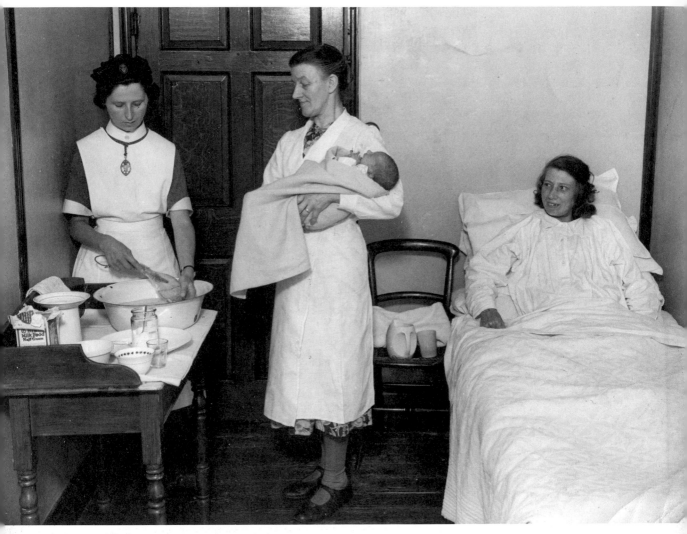

A district nurse on a post-natal visit, 1940s.

training, and wartime certainly tested their ability to rise to new challenges, regardless of where they were working. At home, when the Minister of Labour and National Service issued a clarion call for medical support for essential workers; district nurses and their superintendents were asked to contact the local welfare officers and offer their services in providing immediate medical attention and skilled nursing. Many found themselves assisting in meeting evacuated mothers, children under five and school children at railway stations, then examining them for any health problems that might create a problem with their host family. Head lice were a perennial problem and in January 1940, the district nurses in Bagley Wood, near Oxford, were given the job of examining evacuee children, making 400 visits to the new health clinic, one of many replicated across the country to treat minor ailments. They were also responsible for making eighty-seven visits to check on the suitability of homes the children were billeted to.

Many district nurses assisted in the extra infant welfare centres and ante-natal clinics that were established, whilst others helped by giving lectures and instruction to nursing auxiliaries and members of the British Red Cross Society. One QN wrote of how she was 'loaned' to the London County Council in October 1940 to do work at a temporary rest centre in an East London school which was providing shelter for around 100 people who had been bombed out of their homes.

Her non-nursing duties dovetailed into caring for twenty cases of influenza whom she isolated in a class-room, to attending to children's heads and their general cleanliness, and to making up babies' bottles and dispensing cough mixture. When forty-five badly shocked people needed treating, there were cuts, scratches and lacerations to be dealt with, and days of caring for them as they recovered their equilibrium.

Even the pets who arrived with them - three cats and four dogs - were allowed to stay for one night, before being 'boarded out'. There was no problem recognising the district nurses for a new uniform regulation was soon imposed, and the sight of them wearing a wide white strap across one shoulder and over the back became common-place.

The blackout inevitably caused the nurses some difficulties as autocycles and mechanised cycles could not be used, but to help them be seen in the dark, in early 1940 Messrs. Lunalite of London prepared a:

'luminous armlet ... with the word "Nurse" standing out in bold relief on a blue

Nursing wounded civilians at an emergency centre, where many district nurses assisted. c.1940s.

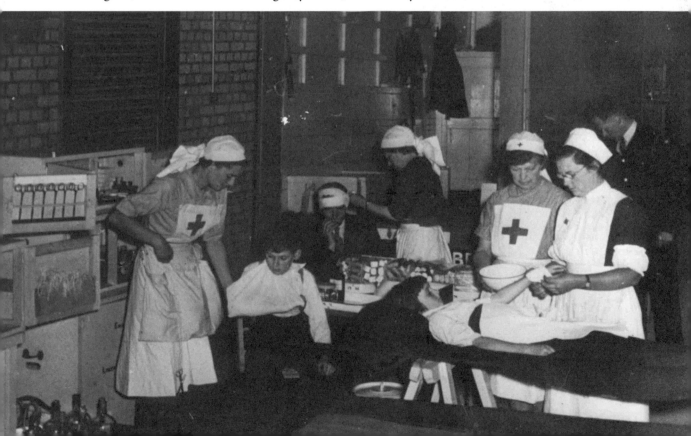

Red Cross nurses and stretcher bearers prepare to transport an injured man to hospital after an air raid. 1940s.

background (yellow in daylight). The price is 1s 6d and 3d postage. Anyone wearing this would be seen easily in the darkness, and nurses visiting in the "black-out" would probably find it an advantage to be recognised in the darkness. The luminous effect can be re-activated by exposure to artificial light.'

For their personal safety, all QNs and midwives were provided with a steel hat and a respirator, but in December 1940, distribution of these items was a matter of some concern with the *QNM* reporting that not every nurse had been provided with these items. At least the gas masks that were supplied were of service quality, which was superior to those issued to civilians, and Bagley Wood DNA even had their own staff air raid shelter.

District nurses, like all other uniformed workers, were affected by the rationing schemes in place, and in mid-1942, the concessions were further reduced, prompting the *QNM* to comment that:

'nurses may feel that the above is a meagre allowance but it has to be borne in mind that the majority of workers have to find all their clothing out of their civilian's coupons and many of them are doing heavy work. We must, do our best.'

In fact, any district nurse who had not registered with the QIDN by 6 November 1942, was unable to get any of the concessions.

Bombing had a devastating effect on many district nursing homes, and it was a great relief that none of the staff were hurt when the one in Coventry was totally destroyed in late 1940. Nevertheless, the problem of starting all over again, whilst continuing to meet the great needs of the community was daunting and caused the nursing association a good deal of anxiety. One of two QNs whose home was demolished during an air attack in a mining area in Kent not only suffered a fractured skull, but lost her mother in the raid. Others all too frequently got caught up in air raids, including Cecilia McGinty in Bridgeton, Glasgow. She was just leaving the district having visited a pregnant patient, when two demolition workers told her there was a man trapped in the wreckage of a tenement on nearby Allan Street. She and two Glasgow doctors bravely made their way through tons of debris to reach the man, who had been there for nearly twelve hours. The only way they could free him was to amputate his foot, and with Nurse McGinty handing up the instruments, Dr Millar performed emergency surgery using torchlight, whilst Dr Ord administered chloroform. Despite their valiant efforts, the man died five hours later. Her gallantry earned her an MBE. Plymouth was another city which was often buffeted and battered by blitz raids, and even though the district nurses were forced to close

North End School in the East End of London, after a bombing raid.

Wartime advert for uniform and rationing allowance list.

the maternity home, they refused to give up on their patients.

The Matron of the DNA was resolute when she said, 'Plymouth people have subscribed for years and we are not going to let them down'. Babies were born as the city was under bombardment, with one mother delivered of her child whilst lying in a narrow passage in the pitch dark, with high explosive and incendiary bombs falling and nearby buildings blazing or crashing to the ground in a heap of ruins. On another occasion, nurses at the Home extinguished incendiaries in their kitchen, two on one part of the roof, and innumerable others on the flat roof of the maternity block. The nurses were quite indignant when the Matron called for male assistance from outside, and by the time six men did arrive, the women had extinguished the fire themselves. Air raid warnings terrified the patients whom district nurse, Sister Gladys, visited in and around the King's Cross area of London. She recorded how one, Mrs Denby, 'just sits in her room during raids and keeps her door open for any neighbour to take shelter with her', whilst another, Mrs Hawkins 'was too nervous to remain in her room and was living in the shelter practically all the time'. Most were worn out from the experience. District nurse, Sister Gladys, not a QN, recorded in her daily notes how she concluded her visit with a prayer and

QUEEN'S NURSES' MAGAZINE.   51

Calling all Queen's and District Nurses

£1000 950 900 850 800 750 700 650 600 550 500 450 400 350 300 250 200 150 100 50

AMBULANCE FUND.

THERE has been a magnificent response from Queen's and other District Nurses for this appeal, and it is hoped that everyone will do their best to secure the amount of £1,000 which is being aimed at, so that the ambulance may be of the best. As the joint Red Cross and St. John Ambulance Board have a good reserve of ambulances, it is suggested that subscribers may like to help the Mechanised Transport Corps, which is composed entirely of women. There are 1,000 members of the Corps, many of whom are voluntary. A contingent was in France until our troops were evacuated, and one is now on its way to Kenya. Those in this country are assisting the military, A.R.P. authorities, Police, Home Guard and are ready to assist civilians if required. They urgently need more ambulances to help in the areas where raids are so frequently taking place. They are also hoping to provide mobile canteens for the Home Guard and others who watch for us day and night throughout the land. " He gives most who gives quickly," so let us all try to raise the £1,000 without delay, and endeavour if possible to celebrate next Armistice Day by making the presentation. The ambulance would bear the inscription, " Presented by Queen's and other District Nurses." You will see how far we have achieved our object by the little picture. We should like this nurse to reach the top before our next issue.

With warm thanks for all who have subscribed and those who will do so.

" There was a man, the world did count him mad,
The more he gave away the more he had."

The *QNM* promoting an Ambulance Fund in September 1940, p.51.

a bible reading. Tales of bravery abounded in the *QNM* and in March 1941 they reported on how Miss Mary Thomas, first nurse in the casualty section of the London Civil Defence Region, had been awarded the George Mcdal. Some months earlier she had crawled through a small hole to administer morphia injections to a man and woman trapped in debris. The report went on, 'the risk was grave, for many tons of debris could have fallen and buried her and the casualties any moment. It was largely due to her courage and persistence that these two lives were saved'.

District nurses in the North Isles of Scotland had their own problems to contend with, as the Scottish Branch report in 1941 pointed out:

'... travelling in the North Isles is always difficult, even in peace time, as one can understand when it is realised how far out in the Atlantic and North Sea some of the smaller islands are situated, but it is much more difficult to say nothing about being dangerous during hostilities. The mode of travel is both ancient and modern and includes aeroplanes, steamers, small craft of every description, motor cars, carts and very often, one's own two feet.'

The nurses had to cope in the direst of weather conditions, and on Shetland in November 1939, nurse Mary Moultrie was snow bound for nearly three weeks, during which time she had two maternity cases to deal with simultaneously. With no other way to get to them, she had to 'plough through walls of snow some eight miles return journey,' and as she was unable to get back to her digs, she spent the night in a neighbouring house. Gales prevented the steamers sailing, and another of her patients, an elderly lady with a fractured femur, had to be taken on a small boat to the ship which called specially to take her to the hospital at Lerwick. Yorkshire was not much better, for a snowstorm forced another district nurse to attempt to walk to reach an expectant mother on a farm at West Scarfton, Coverdale, miles away over the Yorkshire Moors. Called out at 2 o'clock in the morning she became so tired as she struggled through snow deeper than her

2.

HOME CONDITIONS
(TO BE COMPLETED IN THE CASE OF A DISTRICT CONFINEMENT ONLY)

SITUATION OF THE DWELLING (Basement, ground floor, first floor, etc.)	RENT
GENERAL CONDITION (Clean, damp, in need of repair, nature of sanitation, etc.)	NUMBER IN THE FAMILY OF THE PATIENT
	FEE FOR ATTENDANCE AT THE CONFINEMENT
WATER-SUPPLY	NAME AND ADDRESS OF " HOME HELP "
PATIENT'S BEDROOM	SOCIAL SERVICES REQUIRED
NUMBER OF OTHER OCCUPANTS	
PREPARATIONS FOR THE MOTHER	
PREPARATIONS FOR THE CHILD	NOTES

LABOUR

NAME OF THE DOCTOR, IF SUMMONED

Dr Peter Milligan.

CONFINEMENT IN INSTITUTION _____ yes .

CONFINEMENT IN PATIENT'S HOME _____

LABOUR	BEGAN	MEMBRANES RUPTURED	CERVIX FULLY DILATED	CHILD BORN	PLACENTA EXPELLED	DURATION OF LABOUR
DATE	5 . 1 . 42 .	6 . 1 . 42 .	6 . 1 . 42 .	6 . 1 . 42 .	6 . 1 . 42 .	1ST STAGE 29 hrs 30 mins
						2ND STAGE 4 hrs 50 mins.
						3RD STAGE 20 .
HOUR	1 . 30 am .	7 am .	7 . am .	11 . 50 am .	12 . 10 pm .	TOTAL 34 hrs 40 mins

CHARACTER OF THE LABOUR Long 1st Stage
Prolonged 2nd Stage.

USE OF THE FORCEPS _____

INDICATION FOR USE OF THE FORCEPS _____

POSITION OF THE CHILD R . O . A . PRESENTATION OF THE CHILD Vertex

MEMBRANES RUPTURED (a) NATURALLY. (b) ARTIFICIALLY. REASON FOR RUPTURING ARTIFICIALLY At full dilatation

PLACENTA AND MEMBRANES : METHOD OF EXPULSION Fundal pressure.

PLACENTA : TYPE Normal

MEMBRANES : INTACT yes IMPERFECT _____

HAEMORRHAGE : OUNCES : (a) BEFORE _____ (b) WITH _____ (c) AFTER EXPULSION OF THE PLACENTA 3X

LACERATION OF (a) CERVIX _____ (b) VAGINA _____ (c) PERINEUM { INCOMPLETE COMPLETE SUTURED BY Dr Peter Milligan

NUMBER AND MATERIAL OF SUTURES
1 SWG. Suture.

(2)

Pages from Cecile Moore's casebook, whilst she was a pupil midwife in the East End of London.

2.

CONDITION OF PATIENT DURING LABOUR

	FIRST STAGE												SECOND STAGE			
DATE	5/42	5/42	5/42	5/42	5/42	6/43							6/42	6/42	6/42	6/42
TIME	6am	10am	2pm	6pm	8pm	10pm	6am						8.30am	9.30am	10.30am	11.30am
TEMPERATURE	97⁴			97⁸		97⁶	97⁶									
PULSE-RATE	80	84	80	84	80	84	84						84	80	84	84
FOETAL HEART-RATE	140	144	140	140	120	128	124						120	124	136	120
PAINS TYPE / FREQUENCY	W ?1:20	W 1:20	W 1:20	W 1:15	W 1:20	W 1:20	I 1:5						F.G. 1:5	F.G. 1:5	S. 1:5	G. 1:5
URINE PASSED	✓	✓	✓	.	C℥viii	✓	✓									
BOWELS OPEN	.	E.S.	T	E.S.	T	:	.									

SYMBOLS FOR INDICATING THE TYPE OF PAINS : F—FAIR G—GOOD S—STRONG W—WEAK I—IRREGULAR C—CONTINUOUS

NAMES OF ALL PERSONS WHO MADE A VAGINAL EXAMINATION	NAMES OF ALL PERSONS WHO MADE A RECTAL EXAMINATION
Dr R. McMilligan. Miss D. R. Langman.	

NAME OF THE PERSON WHO CONDUCTED THE DELIVERY   Miss D. R. Day & P/R. Moore.

DRUGS ADMINISTERED	DATE AND TIME OF ADMINISTRATION	BY WHOM ADMINISTERED
Ergometrine 1.cc.	6.1.42. 12.30pm.	Miss D. R. Day.

ANALGESIA _____ } BY WHOM ADMINISTERED { _____
ANAESTHESIA _____

CONDITION OF THE PATIENT ON COMPLETION OF THE LABOUR {
TEMPERATURE 97⁶
RESPIRATION-RATE 20
PULSE-RATE 84.
DATE 6.1.42.
TIME 2pm.

REPORT ON THE LABOUR

Mrs de Lilguy was admitted on 5.1.42. at 5am with vague pains ?1:20. Labour progressed very slowly. Hot baths & enema laponis given & proved comforting. Very little diet was taken but patient's condition remained good. Het Sedative ℥i was given 4 hly with some effect. The patient slept for long periods during the night while labour continued very slowly. At 7am the os became fully dilated & the membranes were artificially ruptured by Miss Langman. The patient was encouraged to use her pains to the full extent but they were very short & only appeared at five minute intervals. After five hours in the second stage she was delivered of a living male child. The third stage was normal the placenta & membranes expelled by fundal pressure were complete. There was some loss at the termination of the third stage of labour and I.M.I. Ergometrine 1 c.c. was given with very good effect.

At 2.30pm Mrs de Lilguy was warded in a satisfactory condition

(3)

One of the ambulances bought with money raised by district nurses and presented to the War Office on 18 February 1941, by HRH the Duchess of Kent. The Ambulance Fund raised a total of £4,070.

walking stick, that she had to drag her midwifery bag in the snow. After two and a half hours she had only travelled three miles, and was then confronted by dykes so filled she had to turn back. Just as she was ready to give in, the farmer arrived on horseback carrying a shovel and between them they cleared the snow, rode and walked in turn, eventually reaching the farmer's wife at 6.45 in the morning. Next day, Nurse Shepherd rode the horse seventeen miles to Middleham and back again with medical and other supplies.

The war years impacted on district nurses on the Channel Islands in a wholly different way; they came under German occupation on 30 June 1940, and remained so until the end of the war in 1945. From a tentative start in 1909, when St Helier, Jersey became the first DNA to apply for affiliation, by 1928 there were five associations employing eight QNs between them, and several other district nurses working outside of the organization. By 1939, there were sixteen QNs on the Islands, but one resigned and could not be replaced. Staffing was always difficult, as the pull of the mainland was great, and many well-qualified women were reluctant to make a long-term commitment. They were also reluctant to stay more than two years, because after that time they were completely out of benefit from the national health insurance, and were required to make voluntary contributions. The advent of war in 1939 put a completely different complexion on matters. Miss Bond of the Jersey DNA was desperate for a district nurse by

An East London district nursing home, where two district nurses are checking the patient calls, watched by the superintendent. Note the tin helmets hanging on the rack. c.1940s.

the November, for she was short staffed and 'had lots of babies coming and January is a busy month'. There were no replies to the numerous adverts in the nursing press and by January 1940 the DNA were forced to engage a nurse who only had general training, and no midwifery qualifications. Despite Miss Bond's assurance, in March 1940, that nurses 'had nothing to worry about' the Institute pointed out that the 'nurses are a little frightened about work on the Islands as it is general opinion that it is difficult to reach the mainland owing to the restrictions'. One solution to the staff shortages was to relax the rules, albeit temporarily, by lifting the rule that

Miss Cantrill and Miss McCarthy picking their way across debris left by an air raid on Plymouth to reach the house of a patient, *QNM,* September 1941. p.47.

nurses had to resign if they got married. No one was more pleased than Miss Mulligan, because when she approached the secretary of St Brelade and St Peter DNA in May 1940, expressing her wish to get married but continue working, permission was given on condition that her new status did not 'interfere with her work'.

By 2 June 1940, the nurses had decided to stay put for the time being, although Miss Bond, their superintendent, felt she would 'like to be doing some sort of war work instead of being tucked away in safety'. This place of safety was soon to be turned upside down and as the situation worsened, Miss Bond wrote again to Miss Wilmshurst, the General Superintendent, describing the horror and uncertainty and of how:

'the town is the most nightmarish place you could wish to see, thousands of people are pouring in, and queueing up

A district nurse with her pre-war Austin Seven convertible car in West Hoathly, East Grinstead, 1945.

This picture is one of series commissioned by the Ministry of Information to demonstrate the district nursing training in Guildford, Surrey. Here a trainee district nurse (right) accompanies a qualified district nurse on a home visit. They are greeted at the door by the mother of a young girl recovering from pneumonia. 1944.

By 1948, this district nurse/midwife was being assured that owning a Corgi motor cycle would enable her to carry gas and air equipment easily.

Messerschmitt
—a wonderful friend in sunshine or rain!

You need, for your important work, a car that is completely reliable in all weathers. It also helps if the costs are low. The **Messerschmitt** might have been designed especially for you.

The **Messerschmitt's** exclusive 'tandem' design results in a series of supremely important advantages. First of all—economical performance. Your **Messerschmitt** will cruise happily at 55 m.p.h.—going as high as 65 m.p.h. when the need arises. Yet it gives you this performance at an incredible 87 miles per gallon; and the annual tax is only £5. In fact the **Messerschmitt** is cheaper than going by bus.

The **Messerschmitt** is very easy to drive, and it has one of the simplest, toughest engines ever built.

Your **Messerschmitt** will be a tremendous help in your work. Your patients will benefit from your increased mobility.

Your **Messerschmitt** has the most modern, streamlined shape of all small cars. It is a handsome car to drive—a pleasure to be in, a pleasure to be seen in.

Enjoy a free trial run at your dealer's. There are **Messerschmitt** dealers everywhere, fully equipped for servicing and spares. If you wish to read what independent experts have written about the **Messerschmitt**, send a postcard, giving your name and address to

SOLE CONCESSIONAIRES FOR THE UNITED KINGDOM

CABIN SCOOTERS (Assemblies) LTD.

 Dept. A, 80 George Street, London, W.1
HUNter 0609

The virtues of the Messerschmitt car were being advertised in the *QNM* in 1959.

for evacuation, no method and panic ridden, many of the queued all night … the Bailiff is in charge of the Island as the Governor and his secretary have left'.

Some of the QNs were on holiday at the time of the German occupation on 30 June 1940, which left just twelve of them in post on the Channel Islands. All twelve made a personal decision to stay 'and carry on their duties until further notice'. Neither their DNAs nor the institute exerted any pressure upon them. When Miss Bond heard a rumour that the nurses had left the island, she put a notice in the paper, 'stating that we are still here', and apart from a succinct message, sent via the Red Cross on 29 July 1941, 'All well and carrying on.

REGISTRATION FORM.

Denoting Letter and Number of Place of Issue to be entered here

A 182-17

Two copies of this Form must be completed by every person. If you are in doubt as to how to complete this Form, the Constable or a Douzenier of your Parish will help you.

For Official use only.

No. *1896*

A3

(a) Surname in block letters followed by Christian names. (a) *Young Ellen Jessie*

(b) Ordinary Postal address, including Parish (b) *1 Grange Terrace Green Lane Grange St Peter-Port*

(Au8) 1. Guilles Ter. Mon-Arrivé 26.10.42

(c) Date of Birth (c) *Oct. 29 - 1889*

(d) Place of Birth *Hampton Evesham Worcs.*

(e) Nationality* (e) *English*

(f) Occupation *Professional Nurse*

(g) Single, married, widow or widower (g) *Single*

(h) Colour of hair (h) *Brown*

(i) Colour of eyes (i) *Grey*

As regards question (e), if you are a person possessing dual nationality, give both nationalities

(j) Any physical peculiarities, such as a scar, limp, etc. (j) *no*

(k) Have you served in any of His Britannic Majesty's Armed Forces ? If so, write R.N., R.N.R., Army, R.A.F., Royal Guernsey Militia, or as is appropriate and give your rank on retirement and the date of retirement (k) *no*

(l) Are you on a Reserve of Officers of His Britannic Majesty's Armed Forces ? If so, state which Reserve (l) *no*

(m) Are you, not being on a Reserve of Officers, on the Reserve of any of His Britannic Majesty's Armed Forces ? If so, state which Reserve

	RELATIONSHIP	NAME
(n) Have you a husband, son, grandson, brother, father, nephew, uncle, or first cousin actually serving in any of His Britannic Majesty's Armed Forces ? If so, give his relationship to you and his full name and rank and state which branch (such as R.N., Army, R.A.F., or as the case may require) of the Forces he belongs to. Do not give his Unit or any particulars of his last known whereabouts.		*no*

E.J. Young

If this space for your answer is insufficient, complete your answer on the reverse of this Form.

	RELATIONSHIP	NAME	ADDRESS
(o) Have you a husband, son, grandson, brother, father, nephew, uncle or first cousin who is, to your knowledge, on a Reserve of Officers of His Britannic Majesty's Armed Forces ? If so, give his relationship to you and his full name and address.		*no*	

(p) Having completed the answers to the *above* questions (and where the answer to any of them is in the negative, the word " No " must be written) take this Form to a Constable or Douzenier of your Parish (in the case of Sark, you must take it to the Seneschal) and write your usual signature in his presence and add the date.

(Signature) *Ellen Jessie Young*

(Date) *26/10/40*

Your signature must be witnessed by the Official before whom it is signed and he will sign his name and add his official title and the name of the Parish of which he is an Official.

Witnessed by *H. Guilbert*

(Signature)

(Title) *Cantonal Douzenier, St. Peter Port*

(Name of Parish)

Identity Card issued by _____ (Official issuing Identity Card to insert his initials.)

Star Typ., Bordage.—60m/10/1940.

QN Ellen Jessie Young's official wartime registration form, 26 October 1940. She was appointed QN in April 1923, and worked as a district nurse in Kent, Grimsby and Cheshire before taking up a post with St Peter Port DNA, Guernsey in December 1927.

Hope you are likewise. I miss your visits. Am with you all in thoughts and prayers. Love from Sammy (the dog) and Katherine', there was no more communication with Jersey for four years. Nevertheless, some of the nurses took a huge risk and listened to the news, as Miss Taylor, who worked at St Sampson, Guernsey, revealed in May 1945:

> 'We have had our wireless, a little crystal set which we listened to eagerly for the end of the war. Our other set has been under a haystack since the Germans had them taken from us'.

District nursing carried on during the occupation, but not without complications, for not only did the nurses have to apply to the German authorities to continue their work, but on 22 July 1940, they were ordered not to undertake any maternity cases. This edict was largely disregarded until September 1942, when conditions worsened and home confinements were no longer safe. Some idea of the hardship experienced by the nurses reached Miss Wilmshurst in a letter written by Miss Bond on 19 May 1945, in which she wrote:

The Red Cross food parcels that SS *Vega* delivered to the Channel Islands saved many islanders from starvation. Amongst the last shipment, delivered after the end of the war, were 21,232 standard food parcels, which included American powdered milk, cheese and seedless raisins. *Courtesy of the British Red Cross.*

Children and adults on Jersey receiving Red Cross food parcels at St Helier during the German occupation, 1945. *Courtesy of the British Red Cross.*

'… We have certainly been hungry … No electricity, gas and fuel made it hard, but, when the water was turned off at 8.30 am until 11.30 (sic), nearly did upset us. Last winter was pretty grim for most folk, added to the food shortage. What a boon our Red X parcels have been though we only had them once a month, they did make a change of diet. Vegetables get very monotonous, especially swedes, even they gave out. The old folk suffered keenly but on the whole the children are not too bad. They have been hungry and have eaten plenty of vegetables, resulting in an improvement in teeth, also skin trouble except scabies and in some cases a persistent form of impetigo.'

She also wrote of a diphtheria epidemic in January 1943 and of how Dr McKinstry commandeered QN Miss Thomas for isolation nursing, sending her a general trained nurse as a replacement.

1 Guelle Terrace
Mont Arrive
St Peter Port
Guernsey C. Isles
Channel Islands
22 May /45

Dear Miss Wilmshurst,

Very many thanks to you and your Council of the Queen's Institute for your kind thoughts and interest during the occupation of the German forces. Also many thanks to Queen's Nurse's who have raised money to meet our needs I will do my best not to take advantage of that kind help.

I went yesterday to the film of the Battle of Britain and Desert Victory which tells me all I want to know what the people of Britain have put up with during the 5 years European War.

You enquired what plans I wished to make. I should be very pleased if you can relief me of my Post as Queen's Nurse in St Peter Port Guernsey I am not ill but very tired and need a rest of about 8 months I would like to do some holiday duty of General nursing in a Industrial Town of England for about 6 or 8 months the salary—

would supply my needs to have a rest during the winter months.

We have been well trained under the Nazi Regime so it wont cost much to supply our needs.

Freedom is the most important to me I have not discussed my plans yet with the Committee till I hear from you. When it be convenient for you to send a Queen's Nurse to relieve me, the Military will occupy for 90 days so not much can be done at the moment only for people who are ill. We have been on a reduced salary for 3 years so I changed my address for a Cottage less expensive, with very best wishes to you and all Queen's Nurse's.

Yours sincerely
Ellen Jessie Young.

One of two surviving letters sent by QN Ellen Jessie Young, to Miss Wilmshurst, the General Superintendent, on 22 May 1945.

POST TELEGRAM

Charges to pay — s. — d.   RECEIVED

Prefix 47   Time handed in.   Office of Origin and Service Instructions.   Words.

47 3.20 OF 16 TH GUERNSEY 33

From   To

GENERAL SUPERINTENDENT QUEENS INSTITUTE DISTRICT NURSING 57 LOWER BELGRAVE STREET LONDON W =

= RECEIVED WELCOME RED CROSS ENQUIRY TODAY HOPING FOR REUNION VERY SOON PLEASE NOTE NEW ADDRESS =

ELLEN J YOUNG 1 GUELLE TERRACE +

For free repetition of doubtful words telephone "TELEGRAMS ENQUIRY" or call, with this form at office of delivery. Other enquiries should be accompanied by this form, and, if possible, the envelope.   B or C

Telegram sent by QN Ellen Jessie Young, on 16 May 1945, to Miss Wilmshurst, the General Superintendent. It was stamped 'received' on 19 May 1945.

The practicalities of getting around the island had also caused some problems for early on the Germans had taken Miss Brookes's car, and by the end of the war her cycle tyres were irreparable and all the bicycles were practically worn out. Miss Bond had resorted to solid tyres, which 'for the first six weeks gave me a perpetual headache, but at least it was better than continued punctures. Many folk rode on their rims, on hosepipe if big enough'.

Another QN, Miss Taylor, posted at St Sampson, Guernsey, echoed the sentiments of all the nurses when she wrote of the arrival of the Red Cross ship, SS *Vega*, which brought its sixth and final delivery of parcels on 31 May 1945. It 'seemed like something from an unknown world,' whilst her colleague, Miss Williamson, was thrilled to have 'their first white bread in five years', rather than the staple made with oatmeal, including the husks. On a more practical note, she bemoaned the fact that as a result of the nurses' salary being reduced to £132 a year on 1 July

The British Empire Medal (MBE) awarded to Miss Ellen Jessie Young.

QNs formed the guard of honour on the steps of Lincoln's Inn Hall on 23 October 1945, for the arrival of Queen Mary. Miss Alicia Florence Dickson, SRN, FBCN of the Lancaster DNA, was one recipient of the long-service award, having served for twenty-three years. *British Journal of Nursing*, November 1945.

A group of QNs singing carols at the Queen's Institute, Erleigh Road, Reading, Winter 1946/47. The nurses commented that the winter was one of the snowiest they could remember.

1940, they had 'to sell our treasures and belongings too, to live on black market food'.

More than anything, the district nurses wanted to come home. Katherine Bond's final letter, sent on 6 June 1945, captured her feelings of isolation:

> 'I have suffered from homesickness these last four years as never before in my whole life … I would like to leave about 13 September if travelling is permitted, otherwise I shall only have a winter holiday.'

Unexpectedly, the following day proved to be momentous for the QNs, for the King and Queen visited Guernsey, and at Her Majesty's request, all of them were presented to her. It was, as Miss Brookes wrote, 'a great day for us all'.

As the nation was celebrating the end of the war, so district nurses were being recognised for their valiant efforts and devotion to duty. A thanksgiving service for the 'preservation of

The new uniform seen here came into use on 1 October 1945. There were two styles of hat to choose from, with the new cap, made of navy serge with a rubberised serge covered peak, replacing the old-style storm cap. A new hand-embroidered padded, weatherproof badge was also introduced. *QNM,* 1945, p.83.

Her Majesty the Queen Mother reviewing QNs at Buckingham Palace on 1 July 1946.

QNs' was held at St Martin's-in-the-Field, London on 24 October 1945, with a choir composed of nurses themselves. Numerous QNs were awarded medals for gallantry, including Cecilia McGinty who received an MBE in recognition of services rendered in an air raid in Glasgow. Queen Mary presented Long Service badges to superintendents and nurses of QIDN at Lincoln's Inn Hall on 23 October 1945, and an announcement in the *London Gazette* on 11 December 1945 made rewarding reading, for two of the QNs who had served on the Channel Islands, Miss Katherine Bond on Jersey and Guernsey-based Miss Ellen Young, were each appointed as an 'Additional member of the Civil Division of the Most Excellent Order of the British Empire … for services rendered during the enemy occupation of the Channel Islands'. Miss Bond, Miss Young and their ten colleagues were given a gift of £100 from a fund raised by QNs at home, and, in addition, each was granted £15 from the American War Relief Fund to assist with the necessary replacement of personal belongings.

Chapter 7

POST WAR, THE NATIONAL HEALTH SERVICE AND BEYOND

BY AUGUST 1946, with the war well and truly over, medical care across the country was undergoing radical change, but according to the annual report published in August 1947, the numbers of district nurses were depleted by around 500 to 6,726 of whom 49 per cent, some 3,315, were QNs. Liverpool continued to be a pioneer in district nursing, and became the first DNA to set up a mobile physiotherapy unit. Within five years, the idea had been taken up

An off-duty rural district nurse, weeding her garden, watched by a small boy and two ducks, c.1950s.

A midwife, who was a Queen's trained district nurse, helping bathe a new born baby. 1950s.

by twenty six DNAs, but despite the acknowledged value of the service, it soon become too expensive to provide and was threatened by Ministry of Health cuts. On a more positive note, the maternal mortality rate had dropped to 1 in 1,000, the lowest rate ever, and the midwifery work undertaken by QNs in 1945 and 1946 was considered to have been 'very satisfactory'.

Post-war, another new uniform was designed, and not only were married women now permitted to train and remain working as district nurses, but in 1946, the Ministry of Health instigated an experiment in introducing male district nurses. D.J. Gillett was one of four nurses recruited by the QIDN in 1947, joining Leicester DNA on 31 March that year. He was amused to be regarded as an 'early pioneer,' and whilst he never experienced any gender prejudice, he did hear some women relatives of patients express doubts as to the desirability of men nursing women.

Conversely, some relatives thanked heaven for a male nurse 'because the poor patient is so heavy to manage for any woman'. Mr Gillett recalled his first day on the district:

'…I was taken out by the Senior Nurse and shown the technique of QNs. Nursing in the home, I found, was very different from nursing in a hospital, where the nurse has all the nursing facilities and equipment at hand … Much of the QNs' time and energy is absorbed by cycling from patient to patient. The Male Nurse covers more ground at present than the Queen's Sisters, because he is only permitted to nurse male patients… My average daily travelling distance is twenty-one miles. … During my first six months' training as a Queen's Candidate, I was surprised to find how comprehensive and wide the educational syllabus is. I thoroughly enjoyed my lectures and visits. The lectures included medicine, hygiene, child welfare and management, poor law, charitable societies, local government, diet and Health Insurance, among many others. Visits were made to a dairy where the pasteurisation processes was in progress, to the city sewage works, a Mental Deficiency Home, a Nursery School, a School Clinic, a Child and Maternity Clinic, a large factory (where we were conducted round by an Industrial Nurse), and a Psychiatry Clinic. These were just a few of our varied visits. A complete half day was spent with a Health Visitor. … From my personal experiences, I am sure that the Male Nurse henceforward will become an integral part of the QDNS … District Nursing presents

QNM cover 1947. The magazine was originally published three times a year. It was renamed *District Nursing* in 1958, and became *Queens' Nursing Journal* in 1973 before publishing ceased in 1978.

QNM 1956.

District Nursing, cover, January 1963.

a magnificent opportunity to the Male Nurse to popularise himself and of proving his intense value to the community.'

Leicester DNA soon employed two more male nurses, and before long the scheme was being taken up elsewhere across the country, with Denbighshire reporting that although their male nurse undertook treating many difficult cases at home, most importantly he was instrumental in avoiding hospital admissions. Another male nurse, A.W. Brompton, was keen to dispel the popular idea that male staff were 'purely geriatric nurses', and revealed in a letter to *District Nursing* in 1959 that quite a bit of his work went beyond the call of nursing duty. On one occasion, he wrote of how he spent fifteen minutes in 'taking up a dangerous looking stair-carpet and re-laying it after cutting up the tattered parts'.

Whilst male district nurses were an innovation in 1946, within twelve years, 426 male SRNs had taken up the profession and become QNs. However, their specific requirements were not necessarily being met when it came to uniform, as QN Mr Bell bemoaned in *District Nursing*

Male Uniform
Committee

MALE NURSE

1947-48

QUEEN'S INSTITUTE OF DISTRICT NURSING,
57 Lower Belgrave Street,
London, S.W.1.

PROMISSORY LETTER.

Name ....

Address ....

....

No. on State Reg. ....   No. on C.M.B. Reg. ....

You are hereby authorized to obtain from any supplier the following articles of uniform (and these only).

No. and Type of Article *Annual Replacement*	Maximum Coupon Value	Total Coupon Value
2 short jackets or 1 overall.	5 coupons each.	10
1 pair of trousers.	8 ,, ,,	8
6 aprons or 3 overalls.	4 ,, ,,	24
1 coat or mackintosh.	15 ,, ,, (18 if fully lined).	15 or 18

Initial Outfit		
5 short jackets or 2 overalls and 1 jacket.	5 coupons each.	25
2 pairs of trousers.	8 ,, ,,	16
8 aprons or 4 overalls.	4 ,, ,,	32.
1 coat and 1 mackintosh.	15 ,, ,, (18 if fully lined).	30 or 36

The supplier or suppliers from whom you obtain any or all of the above articles should forward to this address a _____ and quoting the registered number. We shall then forward direct to them the necessary coupons, when the article or articles may be delivered to you.

You should ask the supplier to put _____ his name or stamp, together with details of the types of garments supplied (the number of garments to be made), and the number of [and number] coupons for which he is applying. When all the articles indicated are bought, the letter should be returned to this address, _____

A SEPARATE PROMISSORY LETTER IS REQUIRED FOR EACH FIRM

E. M. CROTHERS,
General Superintendent,
Queen's Institute of District Nursing.

Note.—Details below must be filled in fully by the Firm. Coupon concessions are for one year only and cannot be carried into the next year. Coupons may only be paid three months before delivery of uniform.

Name and Address of Supplier	Articles ordered	Coupons required
....	....	....
....	....	....
....	....	....
....	....	....

L.P.L.—N1997

QIDN promissory note for uniform for a male district nurse, 1948. Rationing was still very much in force, as evidenced by the notes on the numbers of coupons required.

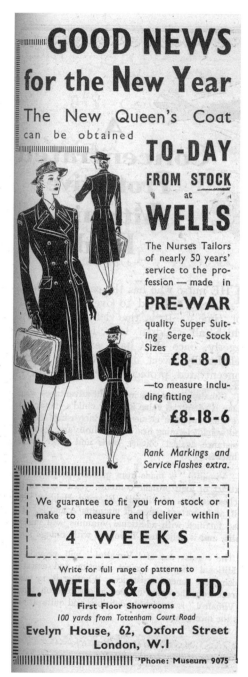

Advert for a new Queen's Coat, *QNM*, January 1947. In 1952, the peaked cap cost 26s 3d, the QIDN Flashes 9s 6d a pair, and a pair of epaulettes, worn by a Queen's Sister, were 14s 0d a pair.

Advert for a new 'Queen's' Austerity Dress, *QNM*, March 1944. Austerity regulations restricted the amount of fabric that could be used.

in September 1958. A new type of bag was proposed for district work and he wondered if 'any thought has been given to the needs of the male district nurse who is required to carry his long white coat with him'. An extra bag was a burden, and he pointed out that bags being carried on autocycles had to be especially durable to withstand the 'great shaking about and general heavy wear'. Raymond Philpot, a district nurse in Somerset, was equally vexed by having to send his uniform to the dry cleaners, and in 1966 begged for 'a working uniform that is recognisable and that can be washed every week'. He was also fed up with being mistaken for the gasman, the electric meter reader and a sailor.

But it was the inauguration of the National Health Service in July 1948 that had the most profound effect on the provision of district nursing services, for this became the responsibility of county authorities. As a way of encouraging people to join their local DNA, a black and white film, *District Nurse*, was made in 1952. Featuring QNs Dorothy Jeal and Nora Parsons, the two women captivated audiences and gave a real insight into the invaluable place of the district nurse in the modern community. It highlighted their daily routine in the village of Wadhurst, Sussex, from home visits, including a houseboat, to attending the local schools, holding infant welfare clinics, organising chiropody and home help as well as hospital visits to discuss a patient's convalescence with the nursing sister. Nurses Jeal and Parsons gave sex education lessons to schoolgirls and ante-natal tuition to expectant mothers, and on rare occasions assisted the doctor with life-saving surgery in a patient's home.

With district nursing now a state scheme, paid for through national insurance contributions, the services of the district nurse were available to anyone who needed home nursing, free of charge. This was a huge relief to many

Male district nurses only put on their white coats once they were in the patient's home, and when a new type of district nursing bag was proposed in 1958, Mr Bell from Lincoln wanted to know if any consideration had been given to storing the white coat he and others wore. c. 1967.

nurses, including Irene Sankey, who trained as a QN in 1941. She had found asking for money, 'embarrassing and distasteful, asking them about their income and expenditure'. However, there were other benefits, for every case could have a district nurse and a doctor if necessary. Although the district nurse was still caring for patients of all ages, many of them were elderly and under the care of a doctor, and the need for special nursing treatment or general care often meant twice daily visits. Here, the advent of better communication, and especially the telephone, played a vital role, and Nurse Evans in Llanfair Caereinion, Wales was not alone in being relieved that at last she was able to get speedy help for the seriously ill, and summon a doctor at short notice. This same nurse had the benefit of a new mobile emergency squad within thirty miles of her. The days of a single telephone in a village were gone, as public kiosks became commonplace and both private homes and district nurses' homes had telephones installed. Some nurses found this quite burdensome, as it often prevented them leaving the home in the morning as they answered innumerable calls. Instant communication was also on the way by the late 1960s with the invention of the car radio telephone.

A male district nurse taking a blood sample from a patient, in the home. c. 1960s.

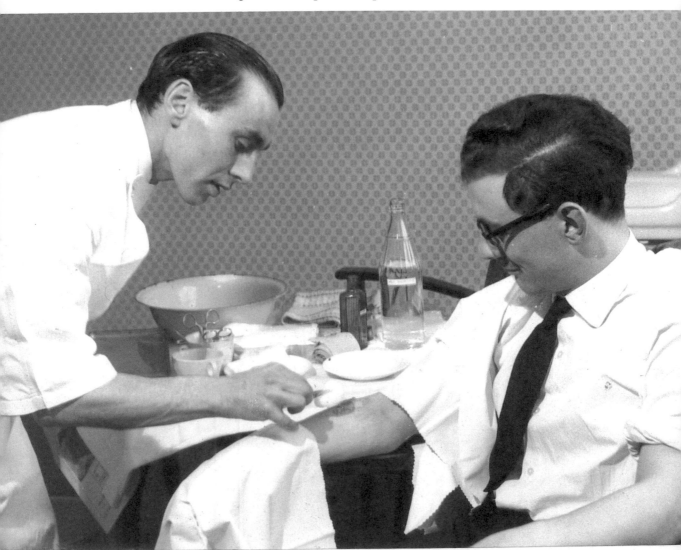

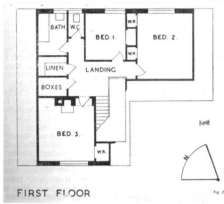

Architect's design for a model nurses' cottage in the Arts and Crafts style. 1949.

First floor plan of a model district nurses' cottage, 1949.

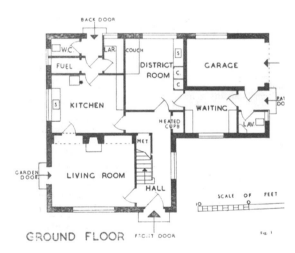

Ground floor plan of a model district nurses' cottage, 1949.

By the 1950s, transport was also undergoing rapid change. As early as 1948, district nurses in Scotland were being given driving lessons during training, a facility which was especially important for rural nurses who very often were unable to get lessons locally.

The increased use of cars made getting around the district so much easier for nurses, and enabled them to cover much larger areas, but it brought with it an increased caseload and less time to spend with each patient. Nurses working for the central London associations were fortunate for as early as 1951, the London County Council loaned them twenty-five cars.

In 1957, Hove and Portslade Association had six cars and two Lambretta scooters as well as two motorcycles and several bikes. Not all the cars supplied were entirely reliable, as Miss Beckie Saunders, a QN working in a rural area in East Sussex discovered in the 1950s and 1960s:

'I did have a car when I went to Lewes to begin with, but I did have to empty every night you know the radiator, and swing it in the morning, it was going out in the night doing that you know!'

As for the QIDN, they were thwarted in their effort to be represented on the Whitley Council, set up in 1948 to negotiate pay. Nor were they successful in gaining control of training, mainly

QN, Geoff Hunt, standing by his 1938 Morris Eight car. He worked in Eastbourne in 1953, and was treating between four and eight patients a day, all suffering from tuberculosis, which was still a killer disease. c.1963.

because they only represented about fifty per cent of practising district nurses, and by 1968 they had withdrawn from training responsibilities completely. Renamed the Queen's Nursing Institute (QNI) in 1973, they had a new patron, Queen Elizabeth the Queen Mother, who took on the role following the death of Queen Mary in 1953. Her Majesty Queen Elizabeth II became the fifth Royal Patron following her mother's death in 2002.

Ironically, as the QIDN was fighting a battle at home with the Ministry of Health to represent district nurses and become a national training body, its influence overseas was growing. This involved the indefatigable General Superintendent, Miss Joan Gray, who travelled the world visiting affiliates and advising governments abroad. In the aftermath of the war, the institute embarked upon a lengthy and complex programme with the Greek War Relief Association of America. The object was to train fifty Greek students as nurses followed by district nursing and health visitor training over a period of four years, so they could return home and start a district nursing service.

Then, in 1946, the QIDN responded to a request from the recently established Malta Memorial DNA to help set the service on its way, and provided a superintendent, Miss Grazier, and six qualified nurses. The Council for Britain made all the arrangements for the nurses to proceed to Malta and their travel costs were met by money raised in Britain

In the mid-1960s, Nairobi City Council expressed an interest in setting up a district nursing service and contacted Miss Gray, the QIDN General Superintendent. There were already some Kenyan nurses being trained in general and midwifery nursing and as the institute had no scholarships available, it was suggested that the Kenyan government might sponsor some of them to undertake Queen's training. Ultimately, Nairobi City Council sent two nurses to England for training, one in October 1965, the other in January 1966.

This district nurse is helping a patient to inject herself. c.1950s.

QUEEN'S NURSES' BENEVOLENT FUND

President : MISS CROTHERS.
Chairman : MISS WILMSHURST, O.B.E.

Hon. Secretary and Treasurer: Assistant Hon. Secretary:
MISS G. M. SEABROOK.   MISS I. M. HICKS.

Secretary-Accountant :
MISS E. IVETT,
6 Park Road, Tring, Herts.
to whom all subscriptions should
be sent.

The object of this Fund is to provide Annuities for Queen's Nurses who are unable to continue their work through permanent illness.

Grants are also given to Members during temporary illness.

Queen's Nurses who have subscribed to the Fund for five consecutive years are eligible to apply for Annuities and Grants if disabled while working as Queen's Nurses. A grant may be given after three consecutive years.

Application for a grant or annuity should be made in the first place to the Secretary-Accountant.

The subscription is not less than 5s. yearly, but more is gratefully accepted; an increase of subscribers means an increase of Annuities.

Since the Fund started in 1913, 239 Queen's Nurses have been helped and 21 are still receiving the Annuity.

Subscriptions should be sent either to the Queen's Visitor or County or Home Superintendent in the subscriber's area, or may be sent direct to the Secretary-Accountant at the above address as early in the year as possible.

To many who have received the Annuity it has meant the difference between being at home and being a member of an institution.

EVERY QUEEN'S NURSE IS STRONGLY URGED TO SUBSCRIBE REGULARLY, AND TO MAKE SURE THAT WHEN MOVING FROM ONE DISTRICT TO ANOTHER, SHE DOES NOT MISS THAT YEAR'S SUBSCRIPTION.

1/4/51

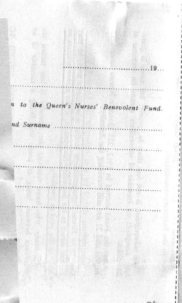

QUEEN'S NURSES' BENEVOLENT FUND

OBJECT. To provide Annuities for Queen's Nurses who are unable to continue their work through permanent illness.

Grants are also given to members during temporary disablement.

The object of the Benevolent Fund, which was set up in 1913, was to provide annuities for QNs who were unable to work because of permanent illness. Grants were also given to members who were temporarily disabled.

Sometimes the remit of the district nurse was nothing if not unusual, never more so than in December 1957, when they were called upon by the Women's Voluntary Service to give talks across the country about what to do in the face of a nuclear attack, as part of the ONE-IN-FIVE scheme set up by Lady Lucas-Tooth. Adaptability was everything, and in the face of an emergency the district nurse could always be relied upon to respond professionally, even when she was off duty. Several trapped people had reason to be grateful to QN Miss Daphne Steer, a bystander on the platform at the time of the Lewisham train crash on 4 December 1957. For three hours she and a doctor crawled through the wreckage to tend victims, with Miss Steer using a borrowed lipstick to mark an 'M' on the foreheads of those given morphia. But it was not just emergencies that tested a district nurse's initiative, as Frances Wright found during her Queen's district training in Birmingham in 1968. Having been accustomed to using sterile dressings and modern techniques, she found herself being shown how to 'make a paper bag out

These QNs are both qualified health visitors, and are running a clinic in the 1950s. *A.J. Knowler /QNI.*

District nurse Jeal weighing a baby at a welfare clinic, 1949.

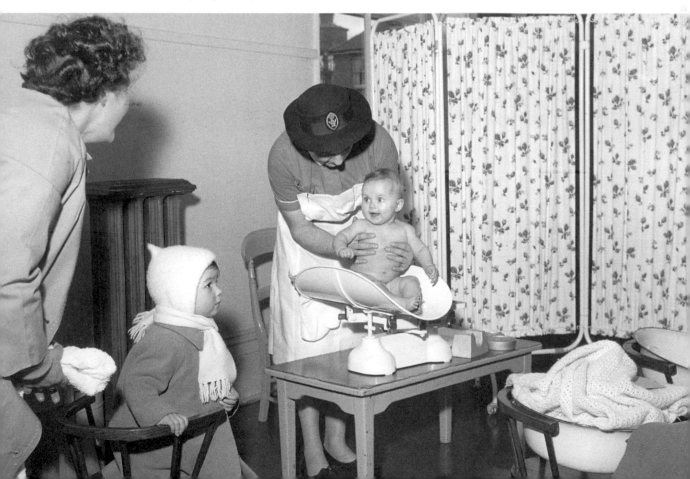

This district nurse is making a home visit to an elderly couple, and explaining case notes to the wife. *R. Saidman/QNI, 1955.*

A district nurse conducting a mother and baby class. c.1950s.

A float advertising the QIDN service, Lincolnshire, 1952.

A district nurse and a general practitioner confer whilst on their rounds. 1959.

of newspaper for the dirty dressings, also we had to take a sheet of paper into homes that were not particularly clean so we could fold our outer coats up and place it on the newspaper'. There were no sterile dressing packs and the district nurses:

'asked the patients to make their own, most people were very adept at cutting up the gauze neatly so no rough edges showed and rolled up the gamgee into manageable sizes then placed them in the large cake tins saved for the purpose. The final task was to bake them in the oven on a high temperature for a period of time (I have since forgotten the details) which was fine until they were left too long and they came out well done and a nice shade of brown.'

Continuity and quality of care has always been at the heart of district nursing and as a way of helping their district nurses manage their time more effectively, Leicester area heath authority developed a computerised record keeping

'Triple Duty Nurse' Katy Shearer visiting local residents in her district at Strachur, Loch Fyne, Argyll between 1948 and 1956. *Courtesy of the Royal College of Nursing Archive.*

A district nurse using her car radio telephone. c.1970-73.

Nurse Jeal writing the details of the patients she was visiting on a slate outside her home. This way she could be reached in the case of an emergency. 1949.

experiment in 1971, which was so successful that it was put into operation in April 1973.

Such innovations, and many more that have been introduced in the ensuing years, have helped transform medical care. The nineteenth century slums may have gone, but poverty and deprivation still exist. Many of the diseases and ailments the early patients suffered from have been replaced by many far more complex illnesses and medical conditions, which have made the job of the district nurse even more challenging. The role of the district nurse has evolved and broadened over the years to provide a wide range of invaluable services in the community, far beyond anything that William Rathbone and Florence Nightingale, the inspirational founders of the profession, could have dreamt of in the nineteenth century. The title of QN, lost when district nursing training was taken over by the NHS in 1968, was reinstated in 2007, and the QNI continues to provide district nurses with free professional support and development. Despite

These district nurses are undergoing training, and being introduced to the structure of the NHS. 1950.

the increase in demand from a growing population for their services, the number of district nurses has dwindled further since the end of the Second World War, but it remains thanks to William Rathbone, whose mission was to provide professional nursing care in the home, and for the new district nurses to see each patient as a whole person, that the profession still exists, for his aims are as relevant today as they were in the 1880s.

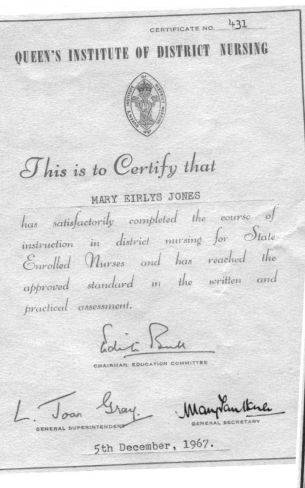

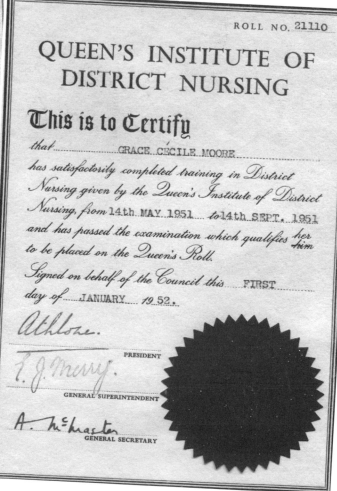

QIDN Certificate awarded to a State Enrolled Nurse, 1967. The majority of QNs and non-Queen's district nurses were state-registered, and some, maybe ten per cent, were state enrolled assistant nurses.

QIDN Certificate awarded to Grace Cecile Moore. According to a Ministry of Health Report, the number of district nurses employed in December 1955 was greater than ever: there were 9,884 in England and Wales, against 9,642 in 1954, and 7,439 in 1947.

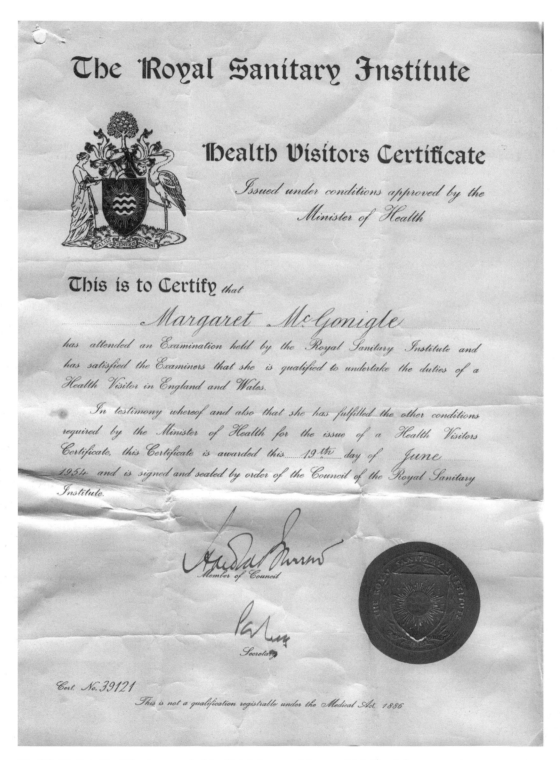

Health Visitor Certificate awarded to district nurse Margaret McGonigle.

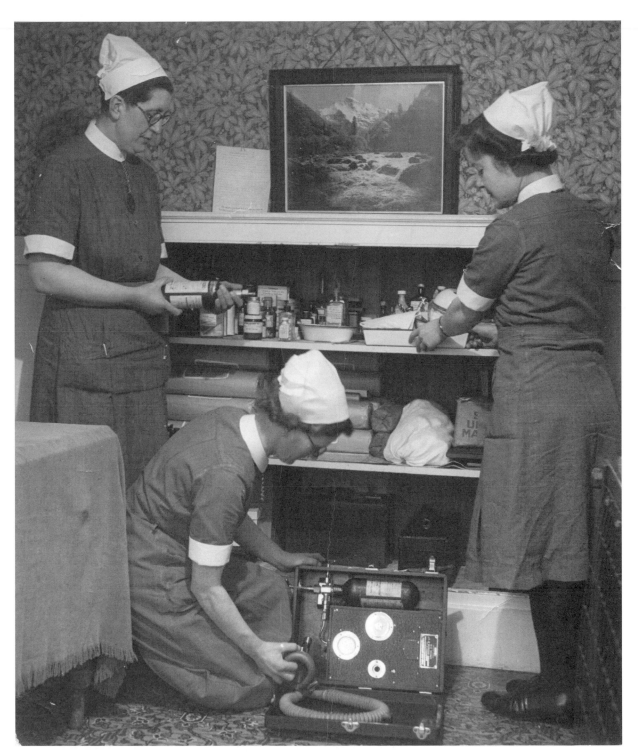

QNs Addison, Dixon and Steele checking their equipment before going out on their rounds.
c.1950s.

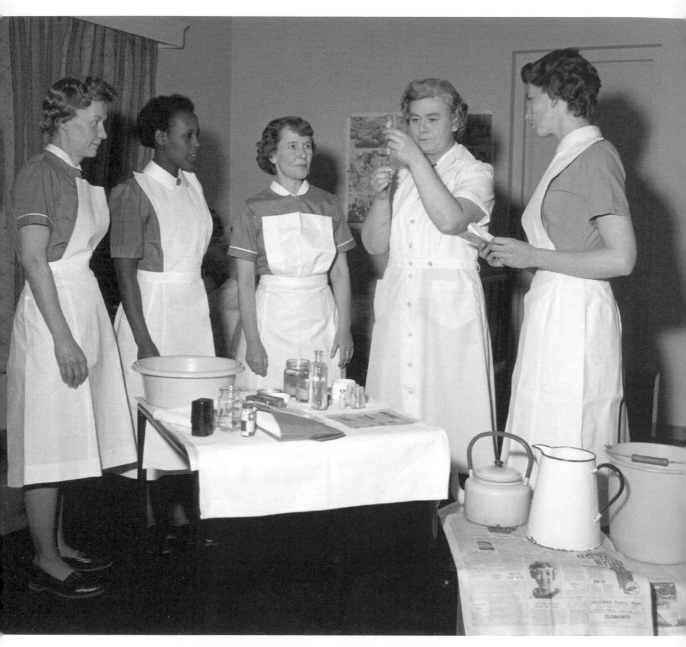

A senior nurse training district nurses in giving insulin injections. c1960s.

QUEEN'S INSTITUTE OF DISTRICT NURSING
DISTRICT NURSES' EXAMINATION

2nd May, 1968

Time allowed for examination : three hours.

IMPORTANT : TWO questions only to be answered in PART I and FOUR in PART II.

PART I

TWO questions only to be answered in this section

1. In what ways can the district nurse co-operate with the hospital staff and family doctors ?

2. What services are available for the elderly housebound ?
   Describe two of the services you mention.

3. Outline the functions of two of the following :
   (a) A Junior Training Centre.
   (b) The School Health Service.
   (c) The Diabetic Association.

PART II

FOUR questions only to be answered in this section

4. When nursing an eighteen month old child with broncho-pneumonia what observations should the district nurse make at the first visit ?
   What advice should be given to the mother on the care of the child between the nurse's visits ?

5. Describe the total nursing care of a man of 46 years with carcinoma of the lung and secondary deposits in the spine.

6. What would make the district nurse suspect that the wife of a patient with a long-term illness was becoming mentally stressed ? What should the district nurse do to help in this situation ?

7. The district nurse is called to a house where a person is lying unconscious. Enumerate the possible causes of the unconsciousness.
   Describe the first aid care of two of these conditions.

8. Describe the total care of a married man of 36 years who has been discharged from hospital after an above-knee amputation following a car accident. He has an appointment at the limb-fitting centre in three months.

Letchworth Printers Ltd.—G7356

An examination paper, 1968.

Nurse Jeal on a rehabilitation visit to a paralysed patient in 1949.

The Greek training scheme created a heavy burden on the QIDN, and did not go to plan. Twenty-two trainees gave up during their training, two left after just a week as they were homesick, whilst the others were variously physically or emotionally unsuitable, worried about their home responsibilities, or simply disinterested.

Miss Gray is being seen off at Victoria coach station, en route to catch a flight from Heathrow to Geneva. She spent two weeks there visiting district nursing services before travelling on to Singapore for the same purpose. 4 March 1957.

A Queen's Nurse boiling instruments in Tanganyika, 1950s.

The Duchess of Gloucester is seen here, on the steps of king's house, Kingston, Jamaica having presented overseas badges to the Queen's Nurses belonging to the Hyacinth Lightbourne visiting nurse service. The district nursing service started work in January 1957, with help from the QNI. c.1960s.

5966

NATIONAL HEALTH SERVICE

This is to certify that

FRANCES ELIZABETH WRIGHT

has undertaken a course of training in

DISTRICT NURSING

at a centre approved by the Minister of Health
and has passed the examination

J.D. Robson

Chairman of the Panel of Assessors

Kathleen A. Raven.   *L. Joan Gray.*

*Chief Nursing Officer of the
Ministry of Health*   *Nursing Officer of Training
Authority*

Date   2nd May, 1968

ROLL No. 33560

QUEEN'S INSTITUTE OF DISTRICT NURSING

This is to Certify that

Frances Elizabeth Wright
has satisfactorily completed training in
District Nursing according to the syllabus
of the Queen's Institute of District Nursing
and on 2nd May, 1968 passed the
examination qualifying for appointment
to the Queen's Roll.

Signed on behalf of the Council.

Alice Mary
PRESIDENT

L. Joan Gray.
GENERAL SUPERINTENDENT

Mary VanKirk
GENERAL SECRETARY

**District Nursing Certificates
awarded to Frances Wright in 1968.**
Courtesy of Frances Tebbutt.

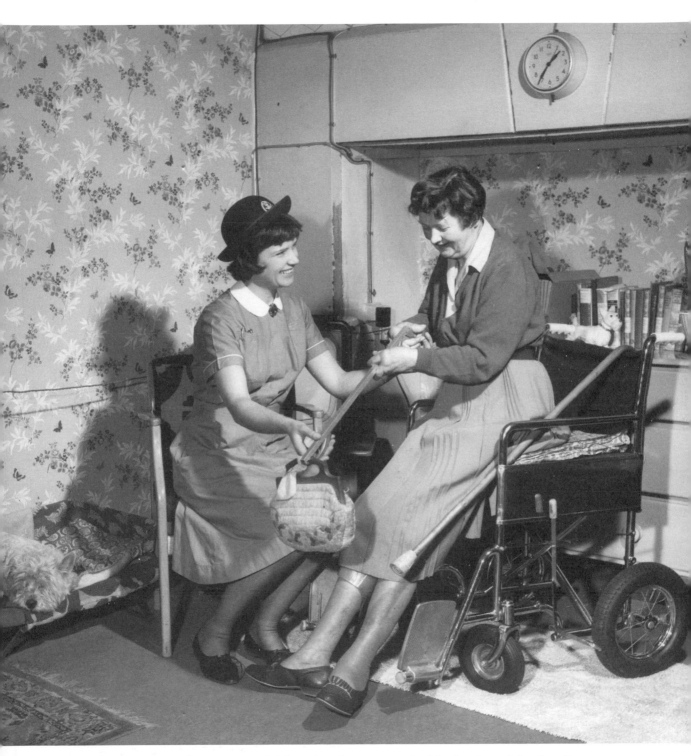

This district nurse is showing an arthritic patient how to use a 'grabber' and reach her handbag unaided. Early 1970s.

This image is of the bombed-out part of Birmingham where Frances Wright worked as a district nurse in the late 1960s. *Courtesy of Frances Tebbutt.*

Southwark DN home, London, opened in 1954.

A district nurse visiting a patient on a council estate in the 1960s.

Acknowledgements and Further Reading

I would like to thank the Queen's Nursing Institute, and specifically Dr Crystal Oldman, CBE, Chief Executive, and Matthew Bradby, Head of Communications, for the help they have provided and for allowing me to use material from the QNI archive. All illustrations are reproduced by courtesy of the Queen's Nursing Institute unless stated otherwise.

Susan Cohen, 2018

BALY, Monica. *A History of the Queen's Nursing Institute: 100 Years 1887-1987*. London & Sydney: Croom Helm, 1987

HOWSE, Carrie, *Rural District Nursing in Gloucestershire 1880–1925*. Cheltenham: Reardon, 2008

STOCKS, Mary, *A Hundred Years of District Nursing*, London: George Allen & Unwin, 1960

The papers of the Queens' Nursing Institute, and other 'historical' nursing related material, can be found in the Wellcome Institute Library and Contemporary Medical Archives, London.

The National Archives website lists the repositories of the papers of very many local district nursing associations.

www.nationalarchives.gov.uk

The Queen's Nursing Institute holds an historical images gallery, as well as information on the history of nursing. 1A Henrietta Place, London W1G 0LZ

http://qniheritage.org.uk

Index